THE POLARIS TRILOGY

Poems for the Moon

Edited by

Joyce Brinkman

Dr. Joe Heithaus

Jessica Reed

Barry Harris

The Sejong Cultural Society
www.sejongculturalsociety.org
606 Forest Road
Glenview, IL 60025

Published by

Brick Street Poetry, Inc.

Photo Credits:

Front Cover: *Polaris A and Polaris Ab* – Original image by ESA/Hubble, recoloring by Joyce Brinkman

Back Cover: *The Lunar Codex / Incandence Corp.*, recoloring by Joyce Brinkman

THE POLARIS TRILOGY

Foreword

ANTARES

I'd been waiting to launch the *Antares* all summer.

The first rocket I'd ever built, red fins swept back at its base like red fletching on an arrow, it stood over a foot tall, an inch in diameter.

I'd selected, instead of an A8-3 first-flight engine, a C6-5 solid-propellant engine. The C6-5 was a single-stage engine, its propellant, delay charge and ejection charge held *in a cylindrical* tube by a clay retainer cap and shaped nozzle—much like the A8-3, but more powerful.

With luck, this baby would lift-off to over 1000 feet.

Next to *Star Trek*, Ray Bradbury and Isaac Asimov, *Estes Rockets* were my passion. They came to prominence by inventing a process for reliably manufacturing small, solid-propellant engines for model rockets.

Estes manufactured a huge variety of kits, ranging from small first-flight model rockets to ones which could house a small camera, designed to take photographs during flight and descent. The fuselages were usually of paperboard, with nose cones and fins of balsa.

It was not just simplicity in design, not just cost consciousness— the construction was calculated to lighten the load under launch, addressing the same issues faced by the main engines propelling NASA's Space Shuttle orbiters.

The first of these Space Shuttle crafts, the OV-101, was intended to be named the *Constitution*; it was changed, after an intense letter-writing campaign by fans of the television series to *Enterprise*.

The *Enterprise* was flight tested atop a modified Boeing 747 aircraft at the NASA Dryden Flight Research Center, and made its first free flight test at Dryden, beginning the cycle that would see humans begin to first use spacecraft that did not have to be discarded after a single flight.

The beginnings, as it were, of a star fleet.

That same year, I stood in a field, electrical line uncoiling from where I was across to the launch pad, where a guide-rod held the *Antares* vertically, facing the sky.

When I threw the switch, the current would race through the line, across the micro-igniter clips to the ignition wire, and the engine would fire with an impulse of 10 Newton-seconds, ramping to a maximum 15 Newtons of thrust in 0.2 seconds, over a total burn-time of 1.6 seconds.

Countdown.

I held my breath.

Now.

THE LUNAR CODEX

The *Apollo* program. The Space Shuttle. Now we stand at the brink of another leap forward, the next small step in humankind's adventure to the stars.

The *Artemis* program is *NASA*'s plan to land humans back on the Moon in 2026, for the first time in over 50 years. It is our first step to Mars.

In parallel, NASA is sending scientific instruments to the Moon, via *Astrobotic Technologies*' and *Intuitive Machines*' commercial lunar landers, launched via commercial rockets built by the *United Launch Alliance* and *SpaceX*.

And we poets – and artists, novelists, essayists, musicians, lyricists, scriptwriters, and filmmakers – well, we will be there as well.

There will be over 30,000 of us onboard in total, in spirit through our poems, paintings, novels, essays, songs, and films, from nearly 140 countries across the globe. These creative works will be etched on nickel-surfaced microfiche disks, or saved in shielded memory cards, carried in time capsules to be archived in perpetuity on the Moon.

This collection of contemporary creative works is the *Lunar Codex*, a passion project that has occupied my nearly every waking hour for the last several years.

The *Lunar Codex* will be the first significant placement of contemporary arts on the Moon in over fifty years.

For me it all began on July 16, 2020, roughly fifty years after humankind first landed on the Moon, and forty years after the first space shuttle tests – and the launch of my *Antares* model rocket.

Astrobotic Technology had been awarded a contract to place a lander carrying NASA instruments on the Moon – and it had opened up commercial payload space on that lander. I reserved enough space to carry what would be my first archival piece, etched on a silver metal disc.

I sourced more payload space on *Astrobotic's Peregrine* lunar lander, loading up my space at no charge with the works of other writers and artists – just wanting to share the joy that I felt. I reserved more space on other spacecraft, including the *Nova-C lander*, the *Griffin* lander, and finally NASA's own *Orion* orbital craft on *Artemis 1*. I began to use other technologies – memory cards that NASA itself used, nickel-based microfiche, bringing onboard with me first 400 creatives, then 1500, then 5,000, and now over 30,000 creative artists.

Slowly, organically, the *Lunar Codex* became what has been called the most expansive, international, and diverse collection of contemporary culture launched to the Moon.

Some have called the *Lunar Codex* a "time machine to the future". Others have called it the "ultimate anthology," and referred to it as a "museum on the Moon".

Significantly, it is the first project to launch the works of women artists to the lunar surface. It includes numerous other firsts, including being the first project, to our knowledge, to place contemporary film and music on the Moon.

The *Lunar Codex* represents creative work from Canada, the U.S., India, China, Australia, South Africa, the U.K., and indeed from 137 countries and territories from Europe, Africa, Latin America and the Caribbean, North America, Oceania, Asia and the Middle East - firsts on the Moon for many of these countries.

And finally, after curating, editing, collecting, waiting – the launches have begun.

On November 16, 2022, the *Orion* spacecraft launched on NASA's *Space Launch System*, to orbit the Moon and return to Earth on December 11, in the *Artemis 1* mission – carrying the first poems from the Lunar Codex, the *Orion Collection*.

Over 2023-2024, the *Polaris*, *Nova-C*, and *Griffin* missions will have launched to the surface of the Moon, carrying more and more works from the *Lunar Codex* to the lunar surface.

The *Peregrine Collection* is our payload associated with *Astrobotic's Peregrine* mission, currently targeted to land in the vicinity of Oceanus Procellarum, near the Gruithuisen Domes, on the Moon.

The *Nova Collection* is our payload associated with the *Intuitive Machines Nova-C* mission, landing in the region of the Lunar South Pole.

Finally, the *Polaris Collection* is our payload anticipated to be launched via the *Astrobotic Griffin*/NASA *VIPER* mission, landing in the Nobile Crater, in the vicinity of the Lunar South Pole.

This latter collection, the *Polaris Collection*, will archive a special book, the one you're reading at this very moment.

POLARIS

The *Polaris* anthology is a singular collection of poetry specifically commissioned for the *Lunar Codex*.

By the time Joyce Brinkman, inaugural Poet Laureate of Indiana and executive director of *Brick Street Poetry*, connected with me, I'd already secured permission from scores of publishers to put poetry collections in my *Lunar Codex* payloads.

When her message came through, I was in the middle of a huge backlog of *Lunar Codex* documentation – but the idea of a *Codex*-specific anthology was especially intriguing. When I talked with her over the phone, I found that Joyce's passion and matched my own – and her connections from a life of poetry put her in a good position to reach out to poets throughout North America and the world.

And so the *Polaris* anthology was born – with Joyce as lead editor, and with the assistance of professors Joe Heithaus of DePauw University, and Jessica Reed of Butler University, the anthology collects the works of over a hundred authors from around the globe, in English and in other languages.

This poetry anthology is a microcosm of the *Lunar Codex* itself, with the voices of creative artists from all over the world joining together an expansive and diverse collection of contemporary poetry.

One day, through the time capsules that make up the *Lunar Codex*, these voices will speak again, and they will speak to the future.

These voices will speak to distant travelers of the richness of our world today.

They will speak to the idea that, despite wars and pandemics and environmental upheaval, humankind found time to dream, time to create.

They will speak to our vison of preserving in the skies some part of our humanity, our art and our poetry, so that when we look up, we might see the Moon as a tangible symbol of hope, of what is possible when you believe.

Samuel Peralta
Founder, *The Lunar Codex*
Toronto, Canada, Earth

December 2022

Editor's Comments

The anthology for the *Polaris* mission is titled *The Polaris Trilogy*. It is an international saga rising from the Earth to the Moon. It tells the story of Earth through the theme words for its three volumes, (Rock, Water, Air,), (Stars, Sun, Moon), and (Ice, Wind, Fire). It tells this story thorough poetry written in the major languages of Earth from all of Earth's continents. It would not have been possible without the vision and work of Samuel Peralta whose foreword proceeds these editor comments.

The call for this anthology did not ask submitters about experiences or degrees, and an effort was made to not view poems through a European/American lens as most world anthologies do. It is inevitable though that responders would not remain untouched by such influence. Although we put out calls in Spanish and Chinese, poets who found those calls were not immune from being influenced by the focus of the European/American lens. Those who don't participate in the view are unlikely to find a call such as ours. There is no good connection point for a world view or even a universal connection point to reaching those immersed in the European/American view.

Given the lack of a universal connection point, it was impossible to accomplish all we wanted to accomplish in the short amount of time we had. A truly comprehensive compiling of authentically written poetry from every country on Earth would be a career's commitment for an editor. Doing so would also have its own disadvantage however. The first submissions would be "history" by the time the last submissions were added and the volume was published. This place called Earth is an extremely dynamic place and it's poetry, like its natural environment, is constantly undergoing change.

By asking for only new, unpublished poems and having such a small window for submissions we have given readers a glimpse of poetry in the first half of 2022. It's an interesting year indeed here on planet Earth. Those Earthlings who are always on watch for the end of time have much to ponder with extreme weather, bringing scorching heat, floods and wildfires. Viruses swirling through the planet, ever changing and every avoiding our best medical science. Rapidly melting ice releasing avalanches and volcanoes belching lava and boulders. Earthlings themselves causing death, destruction and famine with insane wars.

Yet while some of the poems reflect pieces of Earth's struggles there are also those that are filled with beauty, peace and love. Maybe we Earth creatures are just Pollyannaish or we are playing fiddles while Earth burns, but poets seek beauty even in the midst of pain and trauma. Dante has his Beatrice. Even in hell poets cherish beauty.

Because *The Polaris Trilogy* poems are published in their poet's native language there may be no one reader who can read every poem in this anthology. To enjoy the non-English poems please listen to our podcast. Look for "Off the Bricks", where from time to time we will be releasing episodes featuring our non-English-written poems being read by their authors in both the author's native language and English. You can find "Off the Bricks" on your favourite podcast site, and through our posts on our Poetry On Brick Street Facebook page where we announce new episodes and provide a link to our podcast on Spotify. Thanks for reading our printed version. Please listen to the episodes on our podcast and if you ever are on the Moon stop by the Lunar Codex to read some poems there.

Joyce Brinkman, Lead Editor

Acknowledgments

This anthology would not exist if it were not for Samuel Peralta's vision and support. He has my deepest thanks for entrusting me with this part of his spectacular project.

It was a great privilege to read the poems of the many poets who submitted their work. The project elicited energetic enthusiasm from submitters and produced many fine poems that couldn't be used because of our commitment to provide, as much as possible, a balanced presentation of Earth's poetry today.

Thanks to my co-editors, Joe Heithaus and Jessica Reed, for their willingness to support me in this effort. They are dear friends whose commitment to poetry I greatly admire. A special thanks to my intern, Kimberly Owen, who worked hard on the research needed to accomplish this task. Also Corky Benjamin, who is always ready to help. Two students at DePauw University helped with spreading the word about the project. Emilie Prince on social media and Jackson Zhou, who not only has a poem in the book but also provided key help with recruitment of poet and translation of Chinese poetry. A shout out also to Lucy Parks who did the same with the Korean poets and language.

Last, but certainly not least, to Barry Harris Brick Street Poetry Vice-President and the Editor of our *Tipton Poetry Journal*. Barry is always the one I turn to when I'm lost in some aspect of the mechanics of publishing. Barry has an indefatigable commitment to publishing as much of the best poetry as possible. I am grateful for his critical role of serving as our Layout Editor.

Table of Contents

The Polaris Trilogy 2

Stars

Sun

Moon

Together in the Sky

The Polaris Trilogy 3

Ice

Wind

Fire

Together On Earth

PER ASPERA AD ALTA · AD LUNAM ET ASTRA ET ULTRA

ARCHIVED ON THE MOON

LUNAR CODEX™

PEREGRINE · NOVA · POLARIS

WWW.LUNARCODEX.COM

The Polaris Trilogy 1

Rock, Water, Air

haiku to the moon

magic orb up there

silver calm envelopes me

troubles fall away

Margaret Brand,
Belfast, Northern Ireland

Czy to taki twardziel?

Byłem tak twardy

przez miliony lat, chociaż

czasem kruszeję.

Norbert Góra,
Góra, Poland

NEMA VIŠE NIŠTA KAMENA U KAMENU

vremena su postala tako loša i slepa
da ne vidim šta je već dugo oko mene
lagano uzimam kamenje ispred sebe i udaram ga nogama
samo zato što je svet kriv što nemam ljubavi
pa sam postao nesretan čovek

činjenica da mi vreme ne ide u prilog
ja samo bacam kamenje na druge ljude
ne m na sebe ni jedan posto nažalost
i to me košta, jer postajem kameni čovjek

često kažem da u ljudima nema ništa kameno
ali moram znati da je svijet takav
rođen da me iritira po svaku cijenu
samo zato što sam poseban čovek
koji mora biti svjestan svoje situacije

i znam da svijet ne oprašta moja djela
kamen je u prirodi postojaniji nego ikad
sagradio sam svoju kuću u svom okruženju
ali nikada nisam završio svoju
pa zašto još uvijek tražim nešto u svima?

mora da sam postao čovek od kamena
jer kad god želim da čitam za pomoć
ljudi me odbacuju bez stida i stida
svijet je tako čudan i vulgaran dugo vremena
da se ne sećam šta je dan, a šta noć

vrline i mane koje spakujem u jednu stvar
živim svaki dan kao da mi je poslednji
jer shvaćam da sam kameni čovjek ostao miran
zarobljeni u vremenu lutanja k snova
i samo ne želim da budem arogantan čovjek, ali ne ide!

Maid CorbicTuzla,
Bosnia and Herzegovina

Og þegar steinninn fellur

Og þegar steinninn fellur

frá toppi Kaldbaks

Brjótandi allt sem fyrir

verður með brakandi hávaða stjarnanna

Skilur eftir gróp sem verður að á,

svo fiskur,

svo matur,

svo líkami, svo dauði,

svo jörð,

svo steinninn

sem fellur frá toppi Kaldbaks

Helen Cova,
Flateyri, Iceland

Pathfinder

With our rings as round as the "o" in Galileo
We exchange our nuptial vows, our hearts beating
In close proximity. Our hearts' impact once
Scattered regoliths here on the way to Mars.

Poised in awe like the earth-moon spin,
We observe Armstrong and Aldrin's
Fit footprints on the plain's talcum-sands
Then, deftly inscribed by Apollo and Insight.

Further on from the fossil-riverbed, mascons
Spurt all around us like tuberoses. We cannot
See nor touch nor smell these succulents –

Metaphors are maudlin tools on the moon –
Roses cultivated on earth's irrigated soils
Metamorphosed memorabilia of our origins.

Emily Bilman,
Geneva, Switzerland

LLUZ, ESPEYU, SOLOMBRES

Préstame camentar

que los poemes

son l'espeyu au ye reflexada

la nuesa lluz, rellumando

comu relluma'l sol

cuandu acaricia la lluna

(que nun ye namái

un morrillu xigantescu

esnalando pel Espaciu).

Pero tamién camiento

que somos solombres,

porque namái les solombres

son a decatase de la lluz,

solombres allampaes

toles nueches

pola maxa nocherniega

de Selene.

Xe M. Sánchez,
Llanes, Asturies Spain

Water

Long Minutes

Lucca

In the nave of the basilica
Lapped in green and gold
You bathed in the great window's tide.
I loitered to the side among heavy pews
Anchoring myself to a pillar.

Exmoor

By the river Barle
You swam your white hand, wrist deep,
As if the water was nothing more
Than a clean breeze
Floating leaves to the sea.

Home

At the sink you touch a rose
And it is a sleeping baby's ear
In the silver tap-rush
Of a filling vase.

I will always be a rapt bystander
To your long minutes.

Steven OBrien,
Worthing, West Sussex UK

Skin of Water

Midnight catches its breath,
blown over cotton cloud.
Its meditation comes unravelled:
a knot of hair falling in languid descent
down the valley of arched back.
Burnt stars pin the strands of waning,
off the face of the blackened moon.

How the moon enraptures the eiderdown sky,
veiled in sleepless lullaby,
taming stray threads of darkness.

She,
orbiting loneliness,
makes the universe sign witness
as waves are pushed and pulled
on an unmade bed of soil.

Moon peeps around the corner of sky,
wrapped in her silver-cloaked elegy,
conducting the ache and tremble melody
of water's skin
ripped from earthy tongue.

A paper sky dabs away tears,
and for a brief exhale
sighing moon is less alone
in loneliness.
Moon spurns the song of Sun:
her breathing epitaph.
As blinding heart of day rises,
Night falls.

Widaad Pangarker,
Cape Town, South Africa

AUEN
Haiku

Nur die Fils schnattert.

Ich koste mein Alleinsein,

die Blaue Stunde.

*Gabriele Glang,
Geislingen, Germany*

Collide

Resting Sundays in October and the sun does not speak
Rusting spring waters weaving the tide
And the melody teaches dance like music
What a confusion it is that we are taught how to collide in water
Fresh bone and teeth, the masses vomiting them out like litter
The sound of troubled water beaten, tortured waves and hands that
spill ink,
Crescent lips that hung over a mouth full and a cracking moon
seduced by the sands of time
In October, Autumn stung onto bodies,
Carefully sitting voices that mouth words to the sky
Love was honey, a ruling hand sinking with fingers dipped in milk
under a timeless sky
It was not the water that taught us how to make love
It was the sun and sea twisting in a city on fire
In spring time, Sundays got up and left, settling like conscious
sand
and always sinking their eyes delicate waiting for the sun and sea
to collide.

*Londeka Mdluli,
Kovacs student village, South Africa*

Droge Voeten

In dit land met zijn plassen, beken, kanalen, meren,
sloten en rivieren, stroomt water door onze aderen.

Laag gelegen, wachten wij niet tot het nadert, wij zijn één
met de zee, zien onszelf in zijn spiegel, bepalen wanneer,
hoe lang en tot hoever armen mogen reiken.

In dit land met zijn molens, dijken, duinen, dammen, terpen
en sluizen, weten wij wat leven onder de zeespiegel betekent.

We hebben gezien wat verdwijnt als water vrij spel krijgt,
voelden het tot onze lippen staan, de ene na de andere golf
slokte alles op, spoelde voetafdrukken weg.

In dit land met zijn geschiedenis van botters, kotters, fluyts,
kwaks en treilers, leren we al op jonge leeftijd zwemmen.

We leven mee met het water, met zijn verlangen om te stromen,
ruimte in te nemen, begrijpen dat het soms beter is terug te geven
aan de zee, Neptunus gunstig te stemmen en het tij te keren.

In dit land met zijn polders, stormvloedkeringen, wadden
en kwelders is het leven een delicate balans tussen geven en nemen

om onze voeten droog te houden.

Suzanne van Leendert,
Utrecht, The Netherlands

9

A Thirsty Throat

Won't it die without a drink?

What about a dead beast's stink?

Our land is gasping for great greenery

The one that was a cute castle of scenery

Is now a poor, petrifying, parched plainness

The rains forsook the farmers' hopefulness

When they withdrew and played hide-and-seek

With their patient prayers which are purely meek

That's why our land is lacking and drearily dehydrated

The crops cry dry dirges of drooping, none is exhilarated

Ndaba Sibanda,
Bulawayo, Zimbabwe

Ce matin encore

Ce matin encore, pas une ligne tracée.
La nuit se dilue invisiblement
sous la rosée qui vient à ce moment.
Noir de Jais, noir de Mars sont effacés.

La nuit se dilue invisiblement,
encore trop fluide, comme défroissée.
Noir de Jais, noir de Mars sont effacés
dans l'univers profond forcément.

Encore trop fluide, comme défroissée,
ombre sombre, mensonge incorporel…
Dans l'univers profond forcément,
autour, l'océan semble s'arrêter.

Ombre sombre, mensonge incorporel…
Et atteindre les terres éloignées!
Autour, l'océan semble s'arrêter.
Quel horizon? Quel est ce trait de sang?

Et atteindre les terres éloignées!
écrit-il dans son journal, mais il ment.
Quel horizon? Quel est ce trait de sang?
Ce matin encore, pas une ligne tracée.

Catherine Aubelle,
Montaigüet en Forez, France

The Simmering Sea

Although the sea is pulled by lunar reins,
Within a front of servile ebbs, it hides
A fateful pledge once nature's patience wanes
To test its tether with unruly tides.

When frozen hills are stoked by metal fumes,
It brings a rhythmic ruse as billows chase,
For noxious carbon's spew incites the spumes
To lead the charge, when growing flows retrace.

While lies about the turbulence are signs
That battered dams and torrents are ignored,
A steep caress erodes the coastal lines
Amid a unison of spatters roared.

As burgeoning tsunamis stir the straits,
The whirls and quakes engulf resultant wails
While boundless spans cascade at mankind's gates,
And swells accrue the sways of ancient scales.

When swept-up crowds are pleading for an ark
And lands are swallowed by the famished surge,
The moonlit sanctuaries turn to dark
For undulating chains of Gaia's purge.

Daniel Moreschi,
West Glamorgan, Wales, UK

Mediterranean

"...from that Sea of Time,
Spray, blown by the wind." Walt Whitman

There is no music sadder than good-bye, the sound of distant
shores
where I swam my early days, beaches named for distant places:
      Janaklyss, Beau Rivage, Miami, San Stefano.
I knew the sunsets of Alexandria,
soaked with mauve and silver,
      how its swell of waves belied the best divers,
but I swam to an island a mile away,
an only child
      lured by water's song:
          Whatever your journey,
              let's splash an Amen to that.
I told her secrets everybody knows;
how we start in water, how it feels like home.
      I raced the sea floor, learned its dips and swirls,
brought its shells to America,
      till my arms tired of the weight.
Sitting across my days, I raised a conch to my ear,
and an answer rang from its interior:
          I still remember you.

Nadia Ibrashi,
Cairo, Egypt

Fountain

this time she reached
the top and saw
the sun before
dropping into
the pool of her
sisters' arms
who bubbled
and frothed excitement.

to be in the flow
of such clear refreshment
is all she's known and loved.

but now she has felt
the sun pulling her
from herself
taking her
Into unknown
fullness.

this is why
we rush together
cry encouragement
and tears
as we
leap
and push
towards the sky.

Ian Aitken,
Aberdeen, Scotland

Swan Island

Wind waves arguing in angst,
Water flask crushed in those volcanic ash...

Each rainfall led to a waterfall of rain shadow,
Spreading every Zephyr in your memories,

Smashed the Seven Coloured Earths as a pepper,
Each oath taken is an avail of westerlies,

Post your flamboyant departure at sea,
I am a gay swain in a swallowed shamble,
Deep down where lie your shallow shadows...

On the breezeway of the Saint-Géran at seabed,
Is my last heart piece,

I breathe your last air,
You plunge in my last tide...

Scuttled our irrevocable catharsis,
Kedging the last plume of dust,
I water an adieu..

Alshaad Kara,
Mare-Gravier Beau-Bassin, Mauritius

Standing alone with namaste
After Sri Chinmoy at the Vltava

I stand at the river
casting my *namaste*
with my eyes watching without a blink
The floods come often
but never shake my beliefs
Yet, I always return
to *Surya Namaskar*
with my shadow
to whom I have remained a stranger
in all returning suns

The Vltava has tried and failed
in dragging away my reflection

I am the answer
I am namaste
tranquillity standing in bronze
A battle of my reflection and a shadow
ends in each ignoring the other
just as any conflict that resolves nothing
I am a land and a river at odds
And yet a condition of life

I am the water that is only near me
for the light to play and discover tinsel stars
to show one doesn't need skies

My reflection watches the game as *maya*
It is the conjunction of my *namaste*
circling me in water ballet

Yes, I know tides are swelling
But I am not going anywhere

Yogesh Patel,
Morden, Surrey, UK

16

Air

Triomphe mielleuse

Miel sur la langue, cet air d'été,
et iode marin le printemps.

Ça sent jaune des ajoncs
et chèvrefeuille, le soleil levant,
lourd midi, embaumé de roses,

et je suis oiseau, faucon crécerelle,
je lis les motifs changeants,
je perce l'ombre et la lumière,
de voir la vérité oiseau.

Mulot, moineau, n'importe,
je balance dans l'air libre, ailé,
sans jesses ni créance.

Je suis le piqué, triomphe féroce,
et le gout, rouge et chaud,
de tout ce qu'offre la vie—
ce moment, toujours.

Jane Dougherty,
Tonneins, France

The Stench of Poetry

It's half-light in November,
on the school run in go-slow traffic.

A man walks across Erne Bridge,
has a familiar look — the tortured artist.

I try to place where I've seen him before,
slicked ginger hair, beard, black trousers,

It clicks when I see his winter coat
— the blue of *The Starry Night*.

My shout rouses herself from the phone,
LOOK AT THAT MAN!

He's the spit of Van Gogh!
Imagine — Van Gogh in Enniskillen.

She pauses mid-message,
glances out, *Oh yeah! He is!*

There's a poem in this! I say
but herself doesn't miss a tap,

There'll be no poetry in the car.
We'll never get rid of the smell.

Trish Bennett,
Enniskillen, Co. Fermanagh, Northern Ireland

Volare al Sud

Arrivano dal nord stormi di uccelli
riempiendo con i lor canti invernali
filari di magnolie a bordo strada.
Riposano felici nuovamente
col sole che riflette caloroso
dai tetti delle macchine assolate.
Ripetono annualmente quel concerto
fatto di sangue e piume, il loro volo
trasportato da venti evolutivi
li guida scivolando esattamente
dove devono andar, solo seguendo
l'oceano e la vista delle coste.

Blues mamma della terra di Jamaica
fammi ascoltare una canzone adesso
dalle isole tue ricche e volerò
tra nere acque di mari e tra le pioggie
su delle ali d'argento, cavalcando
i venti digitali del progresso
guidata da satelliti stellari
in mano di piloti misteriosi,
verrò portata sulle calde baie,
ad ascoltare il ritmo delle onde –
lasciando nella nostra evoluzione
la formazione antica delle piume.

Lily Prigioniero,
Firenze, Italy

The Wasted Potential of Christmas Trees

Dumped like forgotten New Year
resolutions, you see them thrown
on top of rubbish bags bloated
like stomachs. Others, left on street
corners. Sometimes, groups
gathered in mass evictions.
Some still sport Christmas decorations
gaudy as winter berries - the red and gold
tinsel thin as their trunks. Metallic
baubles round and heavy as a baby beetroot
clinging on for life. The remains
of fallen comrades smashed like broken
eggs lie on the pavement. The fresh,
pungent smell of pine needles long gone.
Trunks close to the colour of freshly tanned leather.
And when you pass one of these trees,
you can only think of a waste of life.
How much air did they not get to purify,
recycle? Was their final breath a small prayer
glowing in the blue winter air or our collective
sorrow gasping for breath?

Christian Ward,
London, England

A Sense of Purpose

The clouds above you form as the moon rises,
you try to give them a sense of purpose.
You know that the messenger with the bad news
won't come, tomorrow, there is no bad news
after this stillness in the world, anymore,
but emptiness.

The lights in the windows not faded away yet, but breathing
and the smile of stars— children, shine. They can smell the wind
more than pets, as you know they prowl the streets, and the smell
of the wind will color them gold.

The storms displace the world without washing us away.
A few centuries pass. The air fills with the same sound,
with the same smell and memories, the sun— love of our life.
In the front yard we see some familiar faces, again,
and the lilac is studded with rays.
The world is lost, but we are young again.
We try to win our life back, we say
thank you past for lessons—
we are ready for future, that is the point
of breathing, many have gone forever,
as in old news, saying a few messages
we don't remember.

Language, the spirit of silence.
Each word, the heart of silence.
Without hearts we are sightless,
with fingers searching for rays.

David Dephy,
Tbilisi, Georgia

[Te acercas sin prudencia hasta el aire y la luz]

Te acercas sin prudencia hasta tu límite,
hasta su exactitud aterradora.
Confín en que podrías despeñarte
por esta sobredosis

de la luz
entrando hasta la aorta que se excede.
Pero entonces no sientes ningún miedo:
no hay corte

ni vacío
ni fractura.
Porque entra en ti la luz y te completa.
Escribe sin ritual, sin expiación,
sin cortejo ninguno del quebranto
y logra derogar la gravedad

de los cuerpos cayendo

hacia su sacrificio de sal roja.

Porque entra en ti la luz y te completa.
Ha de sonar un baile inacabable
en que eres la peonza, el promontorio,
el pubis que remonta de los mitos
para el placer y el círculo completos.

Baila la tierra y quiere ser benigna
como el ojo de un cíclope
que mana llamaradas de alabastro
y las ama deprisa, igual que te ama a ti:
perseida
y pozo.

María Ángeles Pérez López,
Salamanca, España

Luft trug ihn

Mein Bruder lebt nicht mehr
als verblühter Löwenzahn
den er selbst der Erd' entriss, der er entwuchs
um sich vom Schmutz zu trennen

Mein Bruder lebt nicht mehr
      verblühter Löwenzahn

nun gefangen zwischen Daumen und Zeigefinger

Er ist bereit
für einen letzten Atemzug
zu pusten
      Löwenzahn

sät sich hinaus in die Welt

sieht seinen letzten Wunsch
Wirklichkeit werden:

kein Leben mehr

      Löwe

brüllt wutentbrannt in die Welt
im Wunsch, sein Leben wär'
nicht mehr

Svenja Grabner,
Tarrenz, Austria

An Turas

Perched on their seats,
the excited words from them
tumbled our pilgrimage
into childhood's family.
These old neighbours had spotted us
on our long quiet drive; we had not
expected to be remembered.
We had tea, and would have gleaned
a knowledge of the available eggs.
As children,
we would have caught their words,
the unravelling spools of them,
but our own words now
slid between us on our iris-line,
beneath the tall, high windows
of the century-old converted schoolhouse,
that had kept the slope of the hill out,
while those green blades of
agam, agat, orm agus ort,
had fallen in, and got cut not quite away,
into a different kind of owning.
I could only dig, blunt tooled, to the sides,
rummaging well back through my teenaged words,
chipped out for the Cluain Árd ceílí at St Paul's, Belfast,
in what is today, decades later, Ireland's newest Gaeltacht.
Tá pingin dhith orm don fón.
Níl fadbh ar bith. Maith thú fhéin.
Tá sé ag cur. Bhí sé ag cur sneachta.
Dtig liom d'uimhir fón a fháil?
My old Gaeilge words fell to one side.
My Irish subtled English to the other.

Et tous mes autres mots,
ils sont tombés autour de moi.

We had never spoken this language-between,

24

and now we could no longer follow it,
and the spool unravelling thread broke,
and the excitement on the chairs
gave way to slower politeness,
and later into quiet air itself.

Patricia Devlin-Hill,
Belfast, Northern Ireland

VIAGGIATORE

Ero un piccolo essere curioso e con poca memoria

chiamato uomo o qualcosa del genere.

Seduto comodamente su una roccia

dalla riva del fiume guardavo di fronte a me

il punto esatto in cui mi preparavo ad andare.

Cercando di ricordare chi ero o cosa ero stato

dall'altra parte del fiume vedevo la riva ormai lontana

da dove ero arrivato e dove assolutamente non volevo tornare.

Mi misi a cercare qualche oggetto utile per costruire una barca

e una piccola vela che riuscisse a portarmi lontano.

Arrivato incolume sulla terza riva del fiume

c'ero io che mi guardavo seduto impaziente su una roccia

in cerca di un'altra riva che potesse cancellare il fiume.

Ora sono solo polvere addormentata

di colui che fu un uomo o qualcosa del genere

e respiro la dolce aria lunare avvolto dall'universo.

Contemplo il silenzio che mi circonda

e che si riempie di tutte le mie antiche memorie...

Gaetano Longo,
Trieste – Ital

Spinning
Together

On a browning earth, is joy on alien lands?

At the cliff's edge, my gaze seesaws;
here's the sea of our old earth,
Graying like dead skin and unworthy
of poems. I think about the sounds
the water should not make. That folded
clanking and that swish, one dip
and my mouth is sealed tight
and shut off air, packaged and ready
for display at the market or else
for repose with the turtles at the bottom
of the ruin. Onto my back, onto the sky
that is still dry in the months of winter,
that is a shroud thick of smoke
or a curtain shut over a dream; a wishing
star is no longer a phrase. I read
how the air becomes the enemy,
how the earth is a body where soon
we'll choke, like organs expelled. I read
how they look for foreign lands with
clement air, water that rhymes. They look
for a new chance to love. Here the water
is thick like a grudge and air has all reasons
to evade. I roll on my chest again, on my back
again, my gaze seesaws to the avoid
the despair here, by this cliff, that is brittle
and might drop me to the claws of waves,
overlooking smoke dense skies. Over there,
there might be a land, bright. A shooting
star is no longer a phrase; a rock
solid enough for joy to step on.

Amalou Ouassou,
Hassan, Rabat, Morocco

Kamen, zrak in voda

Ko vse drugo odpove,
se kamen, zrak in voda
odpravijo malo na izlet.

Napetost raste.

Kamen se zaveda,
da lahko preseka zrak
in utone v vodi,

zato ostane miren.

Zrak se zaveda,
da lahko prezrači vodo,
a ga kamen lahko prebode,

zato ostane miren.

Voda se zaveda,
da lahko utopi kamen,
zrak pa lahko razburka njo,

zato malo pomisli,
a ostane mirna.

Nihče se torej ne stepe.
Namesto tega sedejo
in zakurijo ogenj.

Zrak zrači kamen,
da se ne vname.

Voda hladi zrak,
da ne izhlapi.

Kamen ščiti vodo,
da se ne prelije.

Imajo vso moč.
Vsa moč gre skoznje.

In zavedajo se:
spet se bo začelo.
Spet se bo živelo

Manja Maksimovič,
Ljubljana, Slovenia

النجم

هكذا هو شارد النجم

رغم أن في تلافيف أناي

إحساس مُترع بجنون العصور

و سم فُطرياتها المُدغدغة لقمم الروح

فبالكاد أُلقي بترانيم العتاب

على تلك الآلات الملقات في عناوين الفُتور

و الذبول في انتظار مصافحة قواطِع الرياح

و ذيول النيران الهوجاء

رغم كل هذا فالبكاد أكشحُ بالعداوة

لذالك الوحش المعاصرالمُنتَصِب على جرف الأسى هناك

فهو على ما يبدوا يتبجح بقبعة التيه فوق عنوان جسده

ومن الفينة و الأخرى يرمقني بنظرات من ترابه

كل هذا و مازلت أقتفي الحب في تمتمة الجنون

قادني طيف لسانه لمعابد الموت

و ها أنذا كالماعز في غفلة و في ذهول

من فرط تقفي الظل و ظل الظل

من شارع تلو الآخر تمر منه بانتظام

مركبات تحمل معها سحنات المحن و التبدد

هذا هو الكل و الكل في هذا الاحساس

حداثة و فقط

مستشعرة على بثور الخضوب

من المفطر للقلب رؤيته

كالمذمم في تجمهر المطر

M. Ait Ali,
Agadir, Morocco

The Moon Song

This locked-on rock of irony
that is our moon:
what's it appear to say if balefully?
Nothing really. It's all in that look.
A cameo of entrance and exit
to what we're about; the me-me of us.
A prop to our mess -a horrified face- Munch
portending what will be on planet Titanic,
the swamping water boring the alleyways
to our cabins wherein we deliberate
what to wear for boat deck's chilly air.
And when we've slipped beneath the ice
the moon will shine its borrowed light
without us to see what's what.

Norman Meharry,
Belfast. N. Ireland

31

Compared To You

Water is the name you give me,
but am I not a tsunami?

Am I not frozen and a gas?
Am I not similar to glass?

Am I not refreshing and high
up in the clouds with the bright sky?

Am I not the flood in your brain?
The thing keeping you almost sane?

Am I not life – whole, full and true?
Or am I nothing compared to you?

Daisy Blacklock,
Cumbria, England

RETURN

The tide has turned its face
from the shore, once more
the herring-gulls feed and quarrel
on the luminous mud
where lonely boats, abandoned and still,
wait, listening for the sound
return of the sea that will come
like the end of a journey.

Upright figures that stand on rocks,
the stranger who digs
for bait or for something he has detected,
the hopes and fears which are his alone.
The rose-blush of air enters
the bay on this invigorating day,
sand-ribbed and rubbed grains
peel away time, a flight of sky
seen before the rolling mist returns

Byron Beynon,
Swansea, Wales

Flow

From sky to earth to lake to river
down, and down and ever down
rippling rills down rocks deliver
ever, never, drink to drown

down and down and ever down
in rapids, stills and ceaseless seething

ever, never drink to drown
these currents to the ocean's breathing

in rapids, stills and ceaseless seething
life abundant, life divine
currents to the ocean's breathing
respiration, life to time

life abundant, life divine
taken for granted becomes scarce
respiration, life to time
is stifled, dying breath in verse

taken for granted, becomes scarce
from sky to earth to lake to river
is stifled, dying breath in verse
which rippling rills down rocks deliver

Ingrid Wilson,
Carlisle, UK

The Bob Dylan Blues

An American Franconian and German Franconian Honour Dylan

1

In your Maggie's Farm as a teenager you heard a gruff voice sing
on the radio.
The fresh air of its imagery struck you like a sharp-tongued
American arrow.
Decades later you read your dialect versions of Dylan songs on
Radio Bavaria..

Doo woor a rauha Stimm im Radio und auf aamoll woor des Dorf
die ganz Weld
a Lied haddmi droffn mid sei Werder, wie a Staa, der wu ins
Wasser fälld
ich woor draußn in am archn Reeng, im Nu in aana ganz annern
Weld

2

I heard Dylan first in college in the early 60s and fell in love with
his vision.
I listened hard to every word and phrase and admired his powerful
precision.
In "Hard Rain" he saw "a dozen dead oceans," "talkers with
tongues all broken."

So vill noochdengd ieber Lieder und Dexde, ieber Gschichdn und
Gstaldn
so vill keerd und gspierd, vo vill verspilld und so vill pfaldn
Zauberschiff woorn in der Lufd, a Wald voller wilda Gstaldn.

3

When news of a Dylan Nobel Prize rode the air waves, we
celebrated in Indiana!
We read immigration poems in the Indiana History Center and
sang a happy hosannah!
That night we savored Dylan songs in the Slippery Noodle Blues
Club, Indy Indiana.

Der Dooch im Oggdober drächd dungle Frichd und helle Freid
ich bin middn in Ameriga und heer vom Bob Dylan seim Breis
a Roggmussiger stehd im Dembl, a Dichder fier unner Zeid.

4
At Jones Beach, Long Island, I heard Bob sing in rain, water
behind the stage and above.
Watching watery waves, I got drenched while he played and sang
the songs we love.
"Girl of the North Country" was so tender I swore he saw his
Minnesota lover above.

In Nämberch, wu die Nazis marschierd sinn und hamm gsunga
wussi ihr Reich fier dausnd Johr in Himml naufheem hamm wolln
hadd verzich Johr dernooch der Bob Dylan gwunna mid seina
Zunga.

5
Mein Bruder, Bob Dylan's work is solid as a rock, but it often
gives us a shock.
We've listened to it together in Franconia and here in Indianapolis,
on my block.
Dylan brought us together, we've laughed till we cried: our
friendship's a rock.

Gedichde hamm uns zammgfiehrd und in Dylan sei Lieder
verbundn
so vill Bladdn und Biecher und Bilder hammer daald ieber die Johr
doo simmer wie Karpfn im Wasser und dreha weider unner Rundn.

Norbert Krapf, Indianapolis, Indiana, USA
Helmut Haberkamm, Spardorf, Germany

The Polaris Trilogy 2

Stars, Sun, Moon

Stars

Stars

5 am

not morning, not quite, stars
still patterned in awakening
sky, cloud-misted, each
alone with its own vast
eternal splendour, or so it
seems to my own longing,
hanging on the edges,
waiting to be born aloft

Kerfe Roig,
New York, New York USA

ꟷꛘꓗꛘꓭꞌꓯ

Mi-k'a-k'e	Star

Wa-zha'-zhe, name of the Osage tribe, . . .who came
from the stars.
Francis La Flesche, *The Osage and the Invisible World*

hu-xia'-ha	Fish scales
thi-bthu'-bthu-xe	tremble
ni-ko-ha	at the edge of the water,
ni o-sho'de	smoky with mud.
no-pe'-hi a-ts'e	Starved,
niu'-mon-bthin –	I walk in the water.
mahka saaki	Blazing star,
ho-co	braided fish,
u-bthi-ge	I catch
ho'-e-ga	in the snare of life.
wáaspe	Stay quiet,
žáa	stay all night.

Elise Paschen,
Osage Nation

38

은하 김홍열

이른 봄 뿌린 꽃씨 봄바람 타고 올라

환상의 밤하늘에 별꽃으로 만발했나.

동화 속 어린 왕자가 꿈을 꾸는 궁전이다.

*어린 왕자: Le Petit Prince

Kim Heung-yol,
Seoul, South Korea

The Whole Universe

We are the star we study
and the star looking back
and the star that is
yet to come
and the star now past

We are even the brown dwarf star
already a planet
on the next horizon
while also wholly in motion
living as beauty;

and still
we are the star
travelling with the ancients
effortlessly deciding
where we will evolve next

forging a new universe.

Hunter Liguore,
Cambridge, Massachusetts USA

The Milky Way

Glittering like a ring of diamonds
over the Continental Divide,
a halo of stars, saints alive,
the summer sky, a gilded shield,
streaked with paint and sparkling stone,
watercolour greens and blues, bands of aurora borealis hues.

A slice of crescent glints,
gold-glazed crumb of lunar cake,
bright in the horizon
as the sprinkles of stars, silver beads
upended from the silk purse of sky.

The mountains pass in reflections like clouds
above the crystalline lake, a cup of world so great
as to hold five planets
seen at once in the sky, this one night,
miniscule satellites,
fingerprints on the galaxy,
touching Neowise, the comet that blinks by
fleetingly, just a pulse, a beat,
a moment too transient to put your finger on,
so exquisite in its brief, magical impossibility
you felt for an instant,
but will never forget.

Amidst this feast for the eyes,
the benevolent heavens, in their song,
symphonic and vast,
so much that is held inside
seems illuminated, alight
as a soaring star,
radiated into the cavernous chasms of space,
echoing,
just as trees speak
through their roots,
their own thread of Morse code,

so, too, do our souls communicate
through the constellations,
ablaze with kinship, hope
in nature's night time skies,
this rambling paradise,
warmed by strings of lights.

Kathryn Sadakierski,
Westfield, Massachusetts USA

Wasted Starlight

Imagine

the feeling as

You formed each individual star, precisely measuring blue turmeric into Vega,

paprika and cayenne for Betelgeuse, sprinkling spinning quasars

while brightening Alpha Centauri, painting galactic clusters,

Northern Lights, aging supernovas to perfection,
and

completing it all with the crown jewel Polaris: a gift

of guiding light, just to see Your people look to the

ground, killing and polluting their perfect virgin world

until they no longer   see the stars, and focus

shifts to escaping,   to find a new

home and   try again

Max Henderson,
Philadelphia, Pennsylvania USA

തമോദ്വാരം

ഒരു തമോദ്വാരത്തിന്റെ ആഴത്തിലേക്ക് ഈ ഗ്രഹം
വീഴുകയാണെങ്കിൽ,
ഇതിനകം തന്നെ മുറിവേറ്റതും, മരണത്തിലേക്ക്
തൊടുത്തു കൊണ്ടിരിക്കുന്നതായിരുന്നെങ്കിലും,
ആരോർക്കുമീ ദുഃഖം,
ബോധതലത്തിന്റെ കളിസ്ഥലം,
അജ്ജെയ്യമെന്ന് നമ്മൾ കരുതിയ,
ജീവനെ പാർപ്പിച്ചിരുന്ന, ഈ ഗോളം?

ഒരു പുതിയ നക്ഷത്രത്തിന്റെ ഉദരത്തിൽ
നാം പൊടിപടലങ്ങളായെരിയുമ്പോൾ,
ആത്മാക്കൾ എവിടേയ്ക്ക് പലായനം ചെയ്യേണ്ടൂ?
അനന്തമായ സുഷുപ്തിയിൽ, അവർ
വീക്ഷിച്ചുകൊണ്ടേയിരിക്കുമോ
ശൂന്യാകാശയുഗങ്ങൾ
അവർക്ക് എത്തിച്ചേരാവുന്ന സമയത്തിന്റെ ഒരു
തലത്തിലേക്ക് മാറും വരെ?

ഒരു ഗസിലിയൻ മൂടിവെച്ച രഹസ്യങ്ങൾ പോലെ അവർ
ഭൂതകാലത്തെ ഒരു ഓർമനിലവറയിൽ ഭദ്രമായി
സൂക്ഷിക്കുമോ,
ഒരു ദശലക്ഷം അസ്തിത്വങ്ങൾക്ക് ശേഷം,
ചരിത്രത്തിന്റെ ഒരേയൊരു ചോർച്ച
സ്വപ്നങ്ങളിൽ മാത്രമാകവെ— ജീവൻ
വേണ്ടത്ര ബോധപൂർവ്വമായ് രണ്ടാമതൊരു അവസരം
കണ്ടെത്തിയാൽ?

ആത്മാക്കൾ കത്തിയമരുന്നവയാണെങ്കിൽ,
ക്ഷോഭിക്കുന്ന നാശത്തിൻ്റെ കൈ കരുത്തിൽ,
നക്ഷത്ര സ്പന്ദനത്തിൻ്റെ കണികകളായി
മാറുന്നതാണെങ്കിൽ,
എന്തിനീ കഥകൾ മണലിലെ രേഖകൾ പോലെ നിലനിൽക്ണം,
അശ്രദ്ധമായി തള്ളിമാറ്റപ്പെടാൻ,
ഒരു അവശേഷിപ്പും കൂടാതെ നീക്കം ചെയ്യപ്പെടാൻ,
ഒന്നിന്റെയും ആരംഭമല്ലാത്ത ഒരു അവസാനത്തിലേക്ക്,
മരിച്ച ഒരു നക്ഷത്രത്തിന്റെ
അപക്വമായ, അന്ധബധിരമായൊരു തരംഗത്താൽ?

Neethu Krishnani,
Mumba Maharashtra. India

Staring at Stars

To assuage fear of dying
I stare at the stars.

Resting on my back, I dream of them
peppering the sky, mysteriously
sparkling on a canopy of darkness
that goes infinitely on.

Then the realization strikes me
that billions of lives prior to mine
had eyes that stared and wondered
at the stars, and died to be part
of all the stardust of which we are
made and brought to life by water.

How each life
peppers time with being
and stares wondering
in the dark at the brightness
of the moon lit by the sun,
and sparkling mysteries
that dot the dark light years away
in sempiternity.

I stare amazed in awe,
but feeling less alone in this mystery.
I can accept my finite life,
as a part of all infinity with all.

I can rest and walk on earth
where our billions of lives reside,
and walk upon the grass of souls,
and feel kinship with all beings,
flying through the universe,
together on one small blue globe
among billions of stars,

each of us a treasure of feelings,
memories, thoughts, and wonder.

Perhaps, *we become birds*

when we die.

Daniela Gioseffi,
Maplewood,New Jersey USA

TIERRA

Aquelarre de estrellas y sombras, el tiempo y su eterno presente.

Encrucijada, el espacio y sus dimensiones.

Apasionada singularidad: la tierra.

En su fecundo regazo,

hijos e hijas nos entretenemos

dibujando signos con secas ramas de olivo;

mutándonos fugaces en ella,

unas veces con parsimonia, otras con furia,

miserias en sueños, heridas en quimeras.

Pensantes y sorprendidos, cruzamos tiempo y espacio

sobre la delicada piel de fuego y agua, roca y viento,

de nuestra única e irresistible morada.

Fernando Cabrera,
Santiago, República Dominicana

Poem of Hope for my Grandson

Every heart in the world
is my heart beating
in his hands.
Liquid stars pour from my eyes
in our video calls
and like a spider
I weave African and Indian
songs into his Taurus hair
hoping the sound of my voice
keeps time with the metronome
of his breathing.
I kiss the air as if it understands
a grandmother's love.
I kiss his eyes through
a glittery screen
and pray this will
all be over soon.
Let this not be the world he inherits.
And it's so hard not to hop
on an airplane,
just to watch him take his
first steps. But I stay home.
Furiously shake
the snow globes of the world
choosing a country,
any country
I want to one day visit
with him.
My grandson and the next, and the next one.
Please come. We will raise
our human flags for you.
As I write. I dream. I surrender.
I practice silence like an art
for him,
this delicate wolfbear boy
who has my heart

has me, a warrior poet,
eating
out of the palm of his hand.
Praying that he will
despite everything
inherit the Lakota stars.

Shonda Buchanan,
On Tongva and Chumash land LA California

운석의 꿈/ 김달호

은하수 길을 따라 이 땅에 오신 손님

함께 온 원자 하나 사랑에 빠졌다가

지구촌 일궈낸 낙원 우주속에 더 푸르다.

Kim Dale Ho,
Korea

I AM A CHILD OF THE STARS

I am a child in the rain
in the sea, in the sky, in the salty air
of a thousand tears and a star.

I am a child forgotten
Remembered, lost, and left
from the stars.

I am a child from the womb of a thousand mothers
in the rain, in the sea, in the sky, in the salt air
of a father's tears.

I am a child in the way
in the room, in the dark, in the night
of the sparkling light
of a star.

I am a child in the light of a thousand fading stars
in the rain, in the sea, in the sky, in the salt air
of an angel's tears.

I am child in the sky
in the night.

I am a child
of the stars.

Oceana Rain Stuart,
Mill Valley, California USA

Tratado comparativo entre el eco poético y la luz estelar

Inspiro y soplo de vida a la nada.
Exhalo y soy el que mueve el universo.

No divago en las bóvedas oscuras,
voy directo al vestigio de las huellas.
Solo las palabras de tiempos viejos
lo presienten,
                vientos enmudecidos
que a veces respiramos, masticamos.
Como luz de una estrella fallecida.
Impalpable epístola del pasado.

La palabra de Novalis en el frío
sigue errante por siglos en el aire,
y yo amarro mi nariz con la correa
y la saco a husmear la noche rítmica.

Nada está lejos en una quimera.
Busco la fosforescencia del nervio,
el hálito que empuña un alpinista
o la atmósfera donde un verso flota.

Arde la emoción y su resonancia.
Las estrellas te queman en sus brasas.
De cicatrices hay constelaciones.
Y es mi familia la noche estrellada.

Rolando Kattan,
Tegucigalpa, Honduras

כוכב

טִפּוֹת-שֶׁל-מְנוּחָה-

יָד-בְּתוֹךְ-יָד-

כָּל-תּוֹשָׁבֵי-כַּדּוּר-הָאָרֶץ-

מַקִּיפִים-אֶת-כַּדּוּר-הָאָרֶץ-

וּמִי-שֶׁמְּחַפֵּשׂ-תְּשׁוּבוֹת-לִשְׁאֵלוֹת-שֶׁשָּׁאַלְתִּי-

אֵי-מֵאָז-שֶׁנּוֹלַדְתִּי-

שֶׁיִּחְיֶה-(אוֹ-יָקוּם)-

פִּתְאוֹם-אֲנִי-מִתְרַחֶקֶת-

זָזָה-

הִנֵּה-צַד-יָמִין-

צַד-שְׂמֹאל-

הִנֵּה-פְּנִימָה-אֶל-הַלַּבָּה-שֶׁלִּי-

הִנֵּה-הַחוּצָה-

לְמֶרְחָב-לֹא-דַּי-בּוֹ-עוֹד-

כּוֹכָבִים-בַּחוּץ-

וַאֲנִי-כְּבָר-לֹא-כָּאן-

וַאֲנִי-כְּבָר-שָׁם-

וַאֲנִי-כְּבָר-

כּוֹכָב-

נוֹסָף-עַל-אֶדֶן-הַיְּקוּם

Lali Tsipi Michaeli,
Tel Avi Israel

THE STAR COUNT

I started to count the stars but had to stop
at twenty. I couldn't keep track of even
those few. They kept rolling around, getting
mixed in among and under and over
the others, like peas in a colander. Look up
and you'll see that selfsame colander,
and maybe feel, as just then I began to feel,
that someone was up there in the darkness,
sorting and rinsing a harvest of stars,
holding them under the cold faucet of time.

Ted Kooser,
Garland, Nebraska, USA

Sun

The Sun as an Axe

The first of us believed the sun
to be an axe swung hard
by a living god, its perpetual arc
both sinister and sweet.

After sleep they gathered
in the rhombuses it made,
for it forgave them and let grow
their scatterings of food. When dark

approached they fled inside
that fear of god once more,
he whose shrouded eyes
would for hours go unsatisfied.

Both wondrous and baleful,
they saw the world the way
they saw their bodies: loving
and destructive, poignant and mean.

They never dreamed of the sun
and never slept when it was seen.
They never spoke of it
except to say it worried them—

like fever in their newborns'
faces, like love's demands
or the risks of red vegetables,
for if they died, it wouldn't.

Carl Boon,
Buca-Izmir, Turkey

现在的我

季佳，河南省郑州市

现在的我

容忍

我的手

像窥视你的眼

容忍 我的心灵

我抚摸你的肌肤

那比落日还要遥远的

神秘的光

正在

一百个夏日的花丛下

颤抖的注视

我的手

而我此时的心

像花丛筛下的 参差的阳光

在明与暗间穿行

一滴花露滴在我

穿行的手上

冰冷的 像我的目光

我的感觉

那是你全部的泪水

Ji Jia,
Zhengzhou City, China

सूर्य

सूर्य तिमी आकाशमा छौ,
तिमी यकदमै सक्ति शाली छौ,
तिमीले हामीलाई तातो दिन्छौ,
तिमी निकै नै टाढा छौ,
तर पनि तिमीले आफ्नो काम राम्रो सँग गछौँ,
उँदाउँमे र अस्ताउँने,
दिन र रातको निमाण गर्दै,
प्रकाश तिमीले दिइरहेको छौ,
तिमी प्रकाश सँग खेलीरहनछौ,
तर त्यसमा हामी तिम्रो पुतली भईरहेका छौ,

तिमी भगवानको यउँटा आँखा होउँ,
तिमी गोलो आकारको छौँ,
मानव पुतलीहरु,
भगवान हजुरले मानव पुतली बनाउँनु भयो,
कसरी हो हजुरको निर्माण भयो थाहाँ छैन,
हजुर जहिल्य पनि दिन र रात बनाउँनु हुन्छ,
हामीलाई हजुरले चलाईरहनु हुन्छ,
हजुरको इक्षामा,
हजुरले जिवन पनि दिनु हुन्छ र मुत्यु पनि,
हामी हजुरको शक्ति देखेर हेरेको हैरै हुन्छन्
तर केही गर्न सक्दैनम,
हामी यउँटा बिना शक्ति भयको मानिस तपरेम ।

विनोद दवाडी
नेपाल ।

Binod Dawadi,
Kathmandu, Nepal

4.6 Billion Years

Scrolling down, reading news of the galaxy. The sun will last at
most another five billion years when it will run out of fuel, become
a red giant incinerating its own planetary system—us. Earth, our
moon, our known fellow-planets and their myriad moons, whatever
else wanders in intergalactic space, vaporized—who cares about
the exact science—it's the fact there's a predictable *kapow* versus
an imagined eternal existence. This puts our solar system's lifespan
roughly at its midpoint, a point my own life can no longer be said
to occupy. Middle-aged galaxy. I'm at the 2/3 point at best, another
30 not-improbable years to go before my own for-sure demise. In
planetary years, I'm older than the sun, a good second half of its
life still ahead, and Earth's with it, barring incoming asteroid or
global self-annihilation. My god, I am older than the sun.

Sally Ashton,
Los Gatos, California USA

해를 안고 오다/ 이광녕

손잡고 새해 아침 에덴동산 타고 올라

빈가슴금빛가득해를안고돌아오니

금실이 곱게 물들어 청실홍실 더 고와라.

Lee Gwang-nyung,
Seoul,Republic of Korea

अच्छी पत्नी सूर्य है (Hindi)

अच्छी पत्नी सूर्य है

कोई शिकायत नहीं

पत्नी कर्तव्य

सुबह से रात तक कोई अंत नहीं

साफ करें, पकाएं, परिवार की सेवा करें

अच्छी पत्नी हंसमुख, खुश, शांतिपूर्ण

अच्छी पत्नी स्वस्थ, धनवान, बुद्धिमान, होशियार

कोई भी पत्नी हमेशा के लिए अच्छी नहीं हो सकती

तो, पत्नी चाकू हो सकती है

अच्छा होने से बचें

बस खुद के लिए अच्छा बनो

Asha Kumari,
Singapore

I Am Circadian Even With My Eyes Closed

Veined like the maranta, I do not pray every night.
my plant raises leaves up in rhythm with the sun,
every cycle the same ceremony. I snip some
branches to propagate, so we can practice
together at the window. sun worshipers
laying down chlorophyll. when day signals,
cortisol must pump. melatonin may cease.
what dreams do you have? flowing root to stem?
painted canvas with water and light.
what night rhymes hum in your network?
if I took you, next morning, to soft marshes
by the docks, would the heron wake you first?
would I find you beneath reeds, whispering
winds that *the sun is coming,* zeitgeber.
gather round. all seagulls hungry for morning fish,
mallards floating in the wake of the hunt,
time-giver. sun ceremony. I shut my eyes,
let down my leaves. depend on you.

Sara Cahill Marron,
Patchogue, New York USA

Epitaph for a Sun
—For JPM

The scarce last words you sealed
with waxy scorn

wrought a silence known

only to the forsaken—

for too long

i too fully believed in
your spurned river's obliteration
in the dusk's ruby mouth
darker than my tear-starved blood
of loss   of chaos

more barren than dust…

Waiting   in my loneliness
for daylight's return

i fitfully slept beside a hieroglyph
etched in red granite…

In the shadows
beneath the artifice
called death
amidst the figurines
of lapis & diorite

i dreamed i was
looking
for you   but
i lost my way
even as Anubis
the ubiquitous jackal
ushered my vague corpse
past intemperate Horus'
hawk-eyes' brackish fire

You were shards

the Curator's censure
had rent from the heavens
& recast in the twilit bronze
of fledgling recklessness…

i leaned against the sunk
relief of a long-forgotten
pharaoh—

until
my sarcophagus opened
&

Then: the name i used to know   *you*

whom i could barely fathom   *were there*
spelled in the cyphers of first light
from the morning's easternmost crest

                    kissing my cheek...

                          Stephanie Harper,
                            Indiana, USA

当我感觉你的手

当我感觉你的手

我想到很多年以前的

那种温柔

其实　你真的不必

以你那冰冷的手

在寒风中与我　相拥

在这个世界

你我原本就是一**种**风景

站在大海与落日的背景下

纯粹成经年的涛声

当我感觉你的手

也许　我不该问你前世

我的今生

但在我写下红尘中

那个欲望的音符时

大海的涛声是否依旧

情有独钟

今夜　你的手是否依旧冰冷

独自站在昨日以前的风景中

应该相信

记忆中的风景不会流年成风

只是今夜 你的无暇令我牵挂

当满天的碎星散尽   那个

为我遮挡由海面吹来寒风的人

在那里……

Wang Denglong,
Chuanhui District,Zhoukou City, China

Fire Of The Past

And just like that with the wind blowing on my face
Your hair behind you like a great golden flame
I fell in love

Your smile and your skin
Dug deep within
The last remaining soft spot in my heart

The road ahead of us
Driving into the sunset
Not knowing what to do next

And its wild
A wild burning passion
The primitive desires of man

And we watched the stars
Then later the sunrise
And it that moment only you and I existed

I could've wanted for nothing else
Even if the whole world had been burning
I wouldn't have noticed

Though it may not have been so clear
I counted myself lucky
When a night felt like a lifetime

Ilias Chafni,
Istanbul, Turk

Moon

failed cartouche

we keep on naming the moon

and she doesn't care,

she doesn't care and still,

we keep naming her, blood

and blue, milk and flower, trying

to get it right, to make something

out of how far away she is,

how she left and cannot come

home, we keep naming her

yet we never see her second face

Daisy Bassen,
East Greenwich, Rhode Island USA

Call Me by My Name

I will answer to *moon,*
my body orbiting yours,
outlining sea and shore and skyscraper
when you call me by my name.
Call me *mahina,*
and I will sink behind exploding mountains,
blossom within coconut palms,
blend into pineapples, flavoring them with yellow light.
Call me *ghealach,*
and I may forget it is not five thousand years ago,
your timeless plains smoothed by glaciers a constant green,
your docile sheep reflecting as whitely
as they have done for eons.
Call me *lua.*
Call me *lua.*
Ask me to illuminate the statue of Christ the Redeemer
and I may balk,
jealous of His glorious light outshining mine.
Call me *Chandra* through the night,
a million voices echoing *"Chandra"*
in poetry and prayer and song
until my craters fill with music
and the Ganges glows
with the deliverance of the dead.
When I am *måne,*
reindeer grunt and pad the forest floor,
their exhalations moonlight clouds
warming herdsmen as they call me by my name.
I am *luna,*
luna when I pull Earth closer to my heart,
and *luna* when lovers gaze my way.
Stars, floating gently out of touch,
chant *"Luna, luna,"*
aching for me to orbit them
instead of the sun and planet I adore.

Jenny Kalahar,
Elwood, Indiana USA

64

LA LUNA

Despierto

Abro los ojos

Es medianoche

Todo es oscuridad

De repente

Una luz se cuela por la ventana

Suficiente para desnudar mi soledad

Siento el frío atravesar mis pies al ir hacia la claridad

Voy al encuentro de algo

Lo siento

Con desesperación aparto las cortinas

La veo

Me sonríe

Está triste y sola como yo

Mi cómplice

Mi compañera

… la luna.

Humberto Quintanar Cinco,
Chiapas, Mexico

Cherokee Moon Prayer

Windy Moon, *Anuyi,* first New Moon
of the season, when we light the fires
of beginnings, turn your face to Earth
as we feed the seeds to soil. Smile
down water and send your sister Sun.

Flower Moon, *Kawoni,* Moon of birth
and buds, give us the herbs and plants
that conjure against Death. Shine on spirit
being, Long Man, as he rules the streams
and rivers where we Knee Deep Dance.

Planting Moon, *Anisguti,* lend us light
as we till the fields, sow the seeds
from season past. Bless the Three Sisters—
corn, beans, squash—as we bury their bodies
in hope of resurrection among sunflowers.

Green Corn Moon, *Tihaluhiyi,* shine with pride
as the corn puts on its silken hair and Earth
wears green with hope that we spread among
our people, lifting up those in need, holding
our elders close as they teach their wisdom.

Ripe Corn Moon, *Guyegwoni,* come celebrate
with us as we thank Earth Mother at the Green
Corn Dance. Do not be afraid of the shouting
and clashing as the Stick Ball players battle.
It is not to the death, just *AniStusti,* Little War.

Fruit Moon, *Galoni,* keep us humble
as we bring in the bounty of tree and bush.
Guide the hands of those who pluck
the plants of wellness, those who harvest
among the heron marshes, beaver ponds.

Nut Moon, *Duliidsdi,* help us pay homage
to *Selu,* First Woman, spirit of the corn.
Let us celebrate Earth at the Brush Feast,
sharing breads made of persimmon, pecan.
Guide our arrows to the heart of merciful hunts.

Harvest Moon, *Duninudi,* you are known
as the Great Moon, you with your golden
face. Beam your happiness upon us
as we give thanks to all we reap from fields
and earth, to all the living that give us life.

Trading Moon, *Nudadaequa,* remind us
of a time before human greed. Let us dance
at the Friendship Festival with those from far,
as we barter our wares. Help us cast upon fire
the transgressions against us, to forgive faults.

Snow Moon, *Usgiyi,* glisten upon the Earth
as She rests in this time of rebirth. In these short
days, throw light onto the ice that clings
to tree and grass. Shelter us as we gather
to hear again ancient stories amid log crackle.

Cold Moon, *Unolvtani*, keep watch as hearth
fires are extinguished and new ones stoked.
In this time of fasting, purification, help us
welcome all new beginnings, salute the arrival
of the morning star in the east, Sun's daughter.

Bony Moon, *Kagali,* join us in the Medicine
Dance. Let us prepare a meal, setting a place
for each of our loved ones now gone to bone
themselves. But do not let us weep in remembrance,
but rejoice in starting over, the new season to come.

Linda Neal Reising,
Cherokee Nation

A bitten moon hangs above winter *

* title from "Ballerinas" by Noelle Kocot

closer much closer even in english
vowels prowl across her pitted face

closer much closer stir the old mumblings
bury your first word for love says the moon

oh the moon dreams of polishing diamonds
the queen can't steal from earth's blue tiara

you're excused bumping into her blind self
third eye busted open by tyranny

oh the moon dreams of crushing impact
oh the moon dreams of forcing poets to feed

her song body sapphires plug nickels hugs
anyone can look at the moon and see

closer much closer even in venus
how much she loves memory her sick dog

JoAnn Balingit,
On Leni Lenape Land, Delaware, USA

달

어머니 떠나신날 올려다본 창백한 초승달

아버지 가신날엔 얼룩진 반달이 내려다보았지

오늘밤 온화한 미소로 저달은 누굴 위로하나?

Lucy Park,
Glenview, Illinois USA

Mid-Autumn
月光
Dazzling in the silky night,
stars paling to the Moon's transcendent
glow shining down on the cement jungle
alight with the technicolor glaze of
Hong Kong.

中秋节

The dried egg yolk center of a glazed
mooncake salts my tongue still heavy with
the rich sweetness of a BBQ bun. I gaze at the
lanterns peppering the sky in golden flame, mind
Floating on the wisps of old amusement and wise
Admonishments from my grandparents at the richly
carpeted, white tables of a dim sum dinner. Red packets
blaze in a flurry of changed hands. A dragon cuts through
the dark, golden fires licking its red belly in a vivid glow.
Incense mingles in the air, thousands of glowing sticks
glittering amongst the crowds. Trees twinkle in the
blue shadows, red and yellow leaves flying down
to rest among centuries-old cobblestone and
ashed incense nubs.

玉兔

Leaping through the stars, friend of the lonely
moon. Your clay figure rests among lime-colored
pomelos, rich oranges bursting at the tongue,
bitter pomegranates grating my throat. A tea
cup rests between my peach-colored hands,
the round moon reflecting its pale gaze
off the dark edge of my tea cup.
Will you jump into my cup?
I peer into the green cup, dark eyes
catching the technicolor glow
this autumn night.

Charlotte Yeung
Hong Kong

69

Apart/Together: Pandemic Night Sky

As always, the elliptical orbit
of you is no star-studded light
show of me, just gravitational
pull between *Wish You Were Here*
and *Here*, blips in the night sky
that synch our breathing. Which moon

best mimics isolation? Of course, new moon
moves in with ancient dirge, orbits
absence while black backdrop of sky
wanes and waxes, its slight punctuations of light
mere crescents of consistent inconsistency. *Here/
Not Here* gains meaning when gravity

gives up its ghost to float us to sky, gravity's
loyalty to earth abandoned for a close-up of moon
and its unromantic glow of distance—*there* to *here*.
Still, memory holds us tight in intersecting orbits.
Half a country away, and the familiar patterns that light
your face light mine. You argue the skies

are different, but really, what matters is not the sky's
design, but the reason we're looking, gravitational
pull still pulling. Despite the miles, lack of light,
weather, terrain, pandemic—moon is still moon
no matter how many times our longing orbits
separate states of being. You *There, Not Here*

defines lonely. But not always. Your *here*
is mine when constellations connect, each sky
enough alike to keep linked even disparate orbits.
This is the way of the body's gravity:
blood pumps, bones grow all because the moon
motions, "Look, follow the tides of light

to love, still here ebbing across this unlit
country of fear." Mark that on the map of *Here/
Now*. So what if the overblown romance of moon

burns cold? What we're viewing each night is sky
that's more than a summary of stars, gravity
the give-and-takes that keeps us each in orbit.

Marjory Maddox
Williamsport, Pennsylvania USA

Esferas

Desde el hogar
mi perra ladra a la Luna.

Aunque estoy envuelto
en mi traje espacial

mi labradora me reconoce

y está esperando
          que le lance
                    su pelotita de hule.

Héctor Carreto,
Ciudad de México, México

A Brother's Love

Sometimes he whispers to me, "I love you to the moon and back."
Other times, he's exasperated. "I'm gonna send you
to the moon!" And still, I'm happy to share our universe.

Elizabeth Jorgensen,
Waukesha, Wisconsin USA

71

La mano sobre la piedra

Yo no era sino un sueño interminable llegado de muy lejos
y soñado muchas veces al mecerme en las lianas del origen.
Nada había demostrado todavía
cuando sapiens me llamaron los que vendrían
milenios después de echar a andar erguido en mis dos pies.
Mis inicios trashumantes fueron fatigosos,
pero alejado del ruido de los días y el cortante
silencio de la noche, casas habité de piedra y agua
donde creció mi descendencia y se dispersó
sin casi darme cuenta por tierras y por mares.
Insinué que había llegado aquí para quedarme
cuando la palma presioné sobre la piedra caliza hasta ablandarla
y dejar allí dibujada la silueta de mi mano, encendiendo así
la luz profunda de la conciencia de mi ser y estar
a través de aquella táctil experiencia existencial inolvidable.
Jabalíes pinté, morosos bisontes y mamuts, ciervos en reposo,
pero también plasmé en la roca la velocidad majestuosa del caballo,
animales todos estos que quería dominar para el sustento
y adquirir su fuerza y los instintos de su especie,
usando el fuego que aprendí de mis ancestros.
De norte a sur anduve, de oriente hasta occidente
buscando cómo hacer mejor el tiempo y el espacio,
la energía inconfundible que había descubierto en mis adentros
y mis alrededores y admirando sobre mí el cielo azul
en donde iban y venían lentamente el sol, la luna, las estrellas.
Todo lo inventé: salud y enfermedad, el habla y su escritura,
mitos incontables de los que muchos forjaron verdades intocables
que hicieron que el conflicto se sentara entre nosotros para siempre.
Subiré a la luna un día y, al igual que en mis inicios, la mano pondré
sobre la roca dura: Yo soy -diré- y he venido aquí para quedarme.

Rei Berroa,
Fairfax, Virginia USA

THE CLINIC

--for JoAnn

Well, the most delinquent among them
break almost instantly, this good doctor for kids
tells me then stops--two, three seconds--
the defiant going first, she said, and it
is like that, a face does shatter like a window.

True, truer in spite of, because of....

She says that as if
her pause can be read as those
nights I looked out of a slow moving car
or past a doorway, up there
the moon's half or its quarter, its beyond
human prehistoric spill
fractured further in the leaves.

She picks up the pieces so carefully that
those young faces keep breaking,
the good doctor holding the fiercest shards
as if catching light really is
how this works. A long minute

until one or the other, she or the child
can bear it, speaking.

She is so kind is not what the kids think.

They think: finally and finally
and lastly, at last.

Marianne Boruch,
Waterville, Maine USA

Electromagnetic Storm

He has learned too late not to turn the radio on,
Even at a low volume, even if just loud enough
For a single person to hear a whisper of tsunami
And meltdown, enduring bad ideas, a past that clings
To a few ragged chords too difficult to whistle.

One person is a world, considering a lifetime
Of conjunctions, disjunctions, ball park errors,
And with that the whole world tunes in,
Even in the dark, and more dark with the clouds low
And unmoving, though there's a hint of moon

Somewhere with its chest-x-ray glow that filters down
As he watches and listens. There's the wind as the car
Races past, bending the reedy grass into the curve
Of an ear that hears every sigh. The night itself
Begs for words to slow its lonely trajectory

Hurtling into space as storyless constellations
Gather around beginnings, stars cocked to catch any word
Of existence, except for the man driving who will not
Turn on the radio ever again. In the morning, he opens
The door and doesn't know, seeing the splintered

Trees, the earth gouged with craters, if he drove
Through another war or a tornado,
But he will always listen to the woman
In the seat next to him who is declaring
She will never speak another word, radio on or not.

Walter Bargen,
Ashland, Missouri USA

Sky Mother

oh Luna
content in your quilt of clouds
do you know *broken*?
I see your scars, your skin cratered
pitted without warning
I trace your molten tears, hardened
a gentle poke - you remain stoic
suspended there in heaven's hush
camouflaged in dapples of pewter
shifting shades of seclusion
nestled deep in night-light stars
you too, have cried

do you know *our broken*?
this world, so worn and whittled
(ass)teroids flailing, (me)teroids amiss
gaining speed without theory
fading fragments of logic, floating
aimlessly to the exosphere
losing control, spiraling to…
Oh Luna, can you catch them?
could you be so kind?
let them steep awhile
in your ebony pools, sun-sodden
heal them in halcyon tides
caressing the grey
of rocks, the grey of life

Michelle Beauchamp,
Sarnia, Ontario, Canada

तुजी सुंदरकाय

तू किदे करपाक शकता जेन्ना चंद्र तुज्या मोगात पडता,
एक पुतळोकसो न्हीदपाचे शिवाय?
चांदीचो उजवाड तुका नाहाणयता आनी कश्टाचो
घाम धुता, काळाच्यो सुरकुत्यो व्हांवून वता,
सपनांक आपलो जीव आसता आनी तीं केन्ना तुटना,
कोण तांका आडवपाक शकना.
तू किदे करपाक शकता
जेन्ना निद्र देवता तुजेर नदर दवरता
तुका अफु दिता, तुजी पिडा
कमी करपाक?
तुका एकवट पळयता
जो मेरेन तुका सुस्ताय येना
तुजे तरणें तोंडाचे कवतूक करता
तुजे धांपिल्लें दोळ्या फाटल्यान
किदें चलता?
तुका किदें दिसता?
तुका खबर आसा हे वर्स खंयचें?
तुका दीस खंयचे रात खंयची ते समजता?
जी बायल तुज्या मोगात
पृथ्वीचेर येता, आभाळातल्यान
तिका तूंय बी मोग करता?
जेन्ना सेलीन (चंद्र देवी) तुका पळयता
आनी लजता, तू किदे करपाक शकता
तिजे खातिर, शांत रावचे सोडून?
न्हीद तुका नेणटो दवरता
आनी मोग तुका सुखि,
अशे तरेन एंडीमियन, तु एक मनीस
पूण तुजी सुंदरकाय
तुका अमर करता.

Akshaya Pawaskar,
Goa, India

l(luna)minated

Luna, our closest satellite,
bathed in light from sol
for eons, its face the same as days of old
one day will shine with man's first torch,
a touch of neon upon its cratered surface.
Illumination signals spacecraft and commerce,
attracting visitors to its empty oceans,
a myriad of habitats surrounds the planetoid.
Lights will guide travelers and adventurers skyward,
reaching tourist attractions and astrobiology labs
through a short weekend jaunt skyward.
Now, we have passed a threshold of progress,
believing our solar powered lights will usher in
a new age of spacefaring, forgetting once more
to admire the mysteries of the darkness.

Angela Acosta,
Columbus, Ohio USA

강촌의 달

눈밭이 희다한들 달빛이 없어봐라
배꽃이 곱다한들 달빛을 가려봐라
강물이 맑다고 한들 달 안 뜨면 뭐하니?

Seo Kwan-ho,
Korea

Me Pregunto

Me pregunto : ¿Me ves de regreso cuando te busco esas noches?
cuando todo es oscuro y se siente más frío
cuando siento un vacío y busco respuesta en tu inmensidad
¿Sabes que existo y que te hablo desde que soy niña?
Esas noches de llanto y vela
noches de entrega a lo que mi alma revela
cuando las emociones emergen desde lo profundo del mar
cuando mi corazón estalla y busca tu consuelo
cuando pierdo el rumbo y me pierdo en la tormenta
Entonces recuerdo que eres un faro
Que guía a los perdidos, a los valientes, a los aventureros
y regreso a las noches de brillo y resplandor
a conmoverme y a estallar de amor
También las noches de celebración
veo tu luz reflejada en el mar
Bailar, bailar sin parar
Al ritmo de tu grandiosidad
Me cobija tu amor incondicional
Siempre has estado ahí
Una compañera leal
Ese faro que me guía
Siempre ha estado dentro de mi
y la luz que veo en ti
es un reflejo y un espejo
del amor que vive en mí.

Natalia Cruz Rión,
México City, México

Self-Portrait as Moon

As always,
I conceal my dark
side, presenting instead
that bright crooked
gleam or my full
countenance beaming
as if in benevolent
approval or even
happiness. Look closer,
you'll find pockmarks
and scars of uncounted
blows. Resignation.
Debris fields invisible
to the naked eye.
No matter which way
I turn, no one sees
the full truth,
the captured whole
suspended there
in solemn grace
and sadness shadowed
by a greater entity.

Robert Okaji,
Indianapolis, IN USA

월광 소나타(Moonlight Sonata)/최 은 희

진통하는 어스름을 털어내는 만삭의 달

사리 밀물 범람하듯 금빛 양수 툭, 터지면

동여맨 치마끈 풀고 에로스를 낳는다

Choi, Eun-hee,
South Korea

Réquiem por mi árbol

La casa donde habito ha sido mi hogar durante más de tres décadas. Sus muros y pisos conocen fragmentos de mi historia. Aquí nacieron mis hijos y murió Glinka, nuestra perra. En silencio, paredes, ventanas y puertas han sido testigos de alegrías y tristezas,

-Y de la vida, no lo olvides, me interrumpe Alter.

-De las vidas, de las muertes, del tiempo vivo hoy, inexistente cuando todo termine, le respondo sentado en una banca en el pequeño jardín de la casa "Me gusta", me digo *sotto voce*, "la presencia de Alter".

La casa no hubiese sido casa sin jardín. Recién llegamos, salvo por el pasto, no había otros habitantes,

Ni enredaderas

ni macetas

ni piedras de ríos

ni limonero

ni ficus

ni patas de elefante

ni floripondios

ni árboles sin nombre

ni lagartijas

ni hormigas

ni sauce llorón

(más bien, mi sauce llorón).

Hace unos días, invadido por muérdago, víctima del deterioro propio del tiempo y de los aires de la Ciudad de México, escuché, atónito, "debe talarse, hay

riesgo de que se caiga", sentenció un experto en árboles, "¿no es posible curarlo?,

¿administrarle alguna pócima?", "no", fue su respuesta. No: dos letras. No: no hay nada contra no. Al día siguiente mi sauce fue talado. Una vida viva menos en mi calendario.

La banca de siempre ya no es igual. Del sauce llorón queda un diminuto vestigio, una suerte de esqueleto: diez centímetros de altura y cincuenta de diámetro. Seco, sin vida. No estuve presente mientras lo talaban. Imposible escuchar el ruido de la sierra, cuyos dientes, lo sé, semejan el ruido de los verdugos.

Sentado en la banca, durante años y años miraba mi sauce. No hablábamos, pero si hablábamos. De noche, cuando el cielo era claro, la luna embellecía el follaje y las ramas de mi sauce. Cuando el viento se apersonaba la fiesta era inmensa. La luna y el viento fungían como coreografía: el sauce bailaba y yo con él.

El viento, la luna y el sauce eran cómplices, hablaban, se reían. De noche, sentado en la banca, o a su lado, intenté escuchar. En ocasiones percibí sus murmullos; fui testigo del amor que se profesaban, trasminaban y contagiaban alegría.

La luna debe estar triste, extraña su presencia. Del sauce apenas queda un fragmento. Parado sobre su base -su corazón- avivo su compañía. Sería lindo hablar con la luna; seguro guarda luto.

Arnoldo Kraus Weisman,
Huixquilucan, Mexico

The Moon and Its Scars

The opulent moon and its silhouette
Does it cast a shadow on you?
Its embalming embrace
and its mellifluous presence
inspired one and many forevermore.

But I'm not an easy target
I cannot be duped easily
I wilfully say,
Not forgetting about the serenade
and the rising aubades
scrivened in your honor.

You, my shifty-eyed moon.
I never forget
my simple mortal breath
cannot leave an impression
on your shiny facade.

Simply existing in your awe
living purgatory of this life
expiating my sins before
going to heaven.
This is the place I truly belong.

A dark shadows
leaking sideways
like a broken yolk,
I can feel the pain
as you hide behind your scars.

oh! my dear moon
I can feel laments in your soul
shining in the milky moonlight
an alleviating embrace;
that you drench us with all.

The moon and its scars
an epitome of imperfect beauty;
heals one and all.

*Megan Sood,
Jersey City, NJ USA*

LUNA INTERIOR

En el cielo del 5 de febrero

ambos, sobre la hierba,

mirábamos llover la oscuridad.

Sus pupilas, voraces agujeros,

succionaban estrellas.

Fue entonces cuando dijo,

(tres años más o menos,

por más señas, poeta todavía)

--*Abuelo, abuelo, escucha:*

suena dentro de mí.

Puse mi mano incrédula

en el sitio más hondo de su pecho

y la oí palpitar, la luna nueva.

*José Luis Vega,
Puerto Rico, USA*

The Artist and His Volcano

To relive the primordial
moment of being slicked out of darkness,
immersed in sensorial radiance,   you must travel
to the artist's mountain in the remote Painted Desert,
        climb its volcanic cinder cone
        into the crater's pitchy tunnel,
                a long dark womb that draws you

toward his steep suspended
bronze stairway—tapering, unrailed
                        lifting you out of the space
                        into the heavens.

Framed in the arc of the rim
        elliptical eruptions of light
                        like a large lucent robin's egg
                        lit from within
                blue ether, mythical constellations, floating moon.

At the crest
                you stagger into the crater's bowl,
                        body   adjusting   resetting
amid strobing pulsations
                earthly   celestial—
clouds, sun, planets—
        shifts of time and space
which you perceive   as only you can
bringing to mind
that first night
you were humbled
                into innocence   drawn into the rapturous sky
realizing you could not hold   the immensity
                                        of space—
        your smallness   its grandeur
so dizzying you raft yourself to a single star,

moored to the blurred line between
connection and isolation
you see everything   know nothing
but the deluge of a mutable sky.

Diane DeCillis,
Bloomfield Michigan, USA

달에게/구충회

지구에서 달에게 이 편지를 씁니다
수십억 년 세월 중 한순간을 살지만
살기가 매우 어렵다는 소식을 전합니다

코비드는 우연히 생긴 병이 아닙니다
인간의 끝이 없는 욕망이 원인입니다
지구가 매우 심하게 오염되었기 때문이죠

생명체가 살기에 달세계는 어떤가요?
인간이 살 수 있는 길을 찾고 있습니다
그래서 우주선 편에 이 편지를 띄웁니다

Gu Chung-Hoe,
Yongin, Gyeonggi-do, Republic of Korea

Moon Shadow

The voids we travel into
willingly, able and fit, afraid
but driven to taste their darkness,
wanting to savour it
fall into them as if
we will be there forever

    That we will build something

But this darkness, this blackness
is luscious enough, is it not?
I can lie within its gentle folds
quivering with the static of time
unending, the pulse of everything
that has come to this point

    in the cosmos

We can hold onto now
as we peer into then, twist
the chains of the static field
as it unfolds across this
southern heave of moon,

    be the explorers
    who come upon this place,
    sherpas of purpose and hope.

Mary Sexson,
Indianapolis, Indiana USA

Sonríen

Norma Muñoz Ledo,
Ciudad de México, México

The Myth of Mother Moon

Snow fell before the wolf moon set
in the pink-hued sky this morning.

Whole and huge moon flanked
by the high-rise and pine trees down

the street. There's a lunacy to the days
leading us to spring. A lunacy

in walking toward the moon in frozen
morning. Fast feet pounding

on slippery wet pavement. Entranced
by imaginary music. Milky mirage.

A distant mother
whole and broken, does not see

her daughter's sun-bruised arms
reach out for her. The ruby-throated

hummingbird never turns
to the moon for comfort.

She savors her nectar
and flies away backwards.

Did poetry make us believe
that the suffering could travel

to nestle and rest in the crook
of our mother moon's neck?

Tonight, we will have clarity. We shall
see her as she is. Pluto in our corner.

To cling tightly to a story, keeps us
in our home's dark cellar. Tonight,

free from devotion, hear us howl
hungry into the blue.

Karen Javits,
Decatur, Georgia USA

Luna sobre la Casa de Bolsa de la Ciudad de México

Luna de provincia
con cara
de recién llegada,
luna hostia
empapada en vino,
luna plato vacío
de los que no tienen casa,
luna de color águila
absorta en devorar
una serpiente
en medio del lago.

Dana Gelinas,
Ciudad de México, México

CINTA BULAN

Bulan purnama adalah dewi kita malam ini

Mummy membawa senjata sucinya pada ziarahnya

untuk melihat kecemerlangan langit yang tiada tandingannya

diam di tengah malam, aku membayanginya

terpesona dengan keghairahannya, terpesona dengan himne ajaibnya

dia dengan malu-malu mengintai melalui ayak

untuk mengelak daripada memandang tepat ke arah bulan

tangan kanan diangkat tinggi

dia melambai kelawar kayunya ke arah bulan

suara merdunya pecah dalam nyanyian khusyuk

bersungguh-sungguh memutar thali, gerakan bulat penuh

kapas yang dicelup dalam kilauan minyak sapi dan berkelip-kelip tanpa

goyah

terletak di dalam cawan tanah liat yang rapuh

dulang perak berkilat sarat dengan gula-gula untuk memikat

besan, barfi, gulab jamun

cinta yang membara di matanya

harapan bersinar abadi

Hari keramat buat isteri

untuk umur Papa yang panjang

dia memberitahu saya untuk menghentikan soal siasat berterusan saya

tetapi siapakah yang akan berpuasa dan berdoa untuk kamu, saya tetap

bertahan?

dia memukul kepala saya dan berbisik

sini, makan barfi

saya tersenyum melihat bulan yang menakjubkan

terbelit lidahku

disalut dengan pemberontakan yang manis

suatu hari nanti, saya akan berada di bulan

Kelly Kaur,
Singapore

신비한 하늘 시집 /박 헌 오

1)
하늘이 들고 나온 손톱만한 노란 시집
책장을 넘길 때마다 떨어지는 은행잎
연못에 떠돌다 만나 시어(詩語)들은 짝짓는다
2)
밤마다 불어나는 책 무거워져 걱정인데
보름날 만삭됐다, 덜어내어 지운 그믐
이듬달 손톱만한 새 책 들고 나와 떠간다.

Park Heon-0h,
Daejeon, Republic of Korea

Moon Phases Zejel

We watch the phases of the moon,
deflated new to full balloon,
from planting time to harvest boon.

Hopeful at the waxing crescent,
youth of moon, an adolescent,
its points of light, iridescent,
but change looms overhead quite soon.

Hail to first and final quarters,
east to west, the sky's cavorters,
made of cheese, or bricks and mortar?
heads and tails of an old doubloon.

Come midway, there's the half of it,
with true reluctance to commit,
light and dark now equally split,
an open mouth to a silver spoon.

And finally the moon is full,
it looks like it's been spun from wool,
on tides, it rends a massive pull,
and wraps the night in its cocoon.

Cynthia Gallaher,
Chicago, Illinois USA

I note the constellations, but my grandson is stuck on cars.

Eyes only for trikes and bikes, drivers, haulers, trucker shows. Then,

"Look, the moon!" He points, enchanted. "Like a glowing, giant wheel."

Nancy Jorgensen,
Waukesha, Wisconsin USA

An Ode to the Moon and Those Who Helped Us Arrive

The Dream　　　　**and**　　　　**Now**

One
Wonderful　　　　　　　　Look at this
Moment　　　Shows us a　　　Luminous moon
Finds us　　　Hoping　　　Finds an astonishing reality
Lifting our gaze　　To the sky above　　We're walking on you
Dreaming like children　Flying flags and　　　Soaring high
Standing on the shoulders　　　On the accumulated accomplishments
Of those that tired but tried again　Progressing from　The gains of generations
Looking to the future　　And finding that the future　Started so many yesterdays ago
Wondering what is the price to pay and what will be the final prize　　　What is
Yet to come in this spectacle and　　What is　　　　　　Found
What surprises wait　　While dreaming of you　　When boundaries are burst
Flying to you　　To now know what is possible　Where we were unable to stand
From a rotating rock's　　Earthly connection　　　　Beyond the
Reflections　　　Through space to the　　Previously unreachable
Now shining on your face　After being held down by something lighter than wind　Through space
So we can see　That as it turns out, we can cross through the empty dark　　To see
The man on the moon　　　Surviving and　　　　What is driving us
We realize　　Watching you wax and wane that　　　Now
|　Still as the stone　That some stand on you while most of us view you　From afar
Out in space　　　Here　Or where we reside beside or on you
In silence　Sounds unable to penetrate　Through the vast vacuum of space
What goes on in the night　Earthbound no more　We see what comes to light
We are thinking about the time　Till some find　Ours is not a flightless fate
We will not see you　　　　　　Instead
We will only see　　That　We find we were
We are connected

Mike Nierste,
Zionsville, Indiana USA

93

Together in the Sky

Without even getting out of bed

I cannot be bored with so much
world at hand: day slides in and out
of night; stars make room for moon
who yields to sun; clouds and other shadows
play through leaves, over the counterpane.
What more awaits me when I I rise?

Jennifer Barricklow,
Lexington, Kentucky USA

Light and shadow

I rise, invited by its light.

It bids me welcome and breathes,

inhaling cherry blossoms,
whispering,

on the back of my neck

airborne words:

lunar, craters, and tide.

Come, it tells me

in a *TREMULOUS* voice,

look for me among the tops

of buildings and trees,
amid fierce horns

and the whistle of the *tamalero*.
Look for me and you will find
the hidden side of your sun

Me levanto invitada por su luz
Me acoge y respira
inhala flores de cerezo
susurra en mi nuca
palabras aéreas

mareas cráteres lunar.
Anda, me dice,
la voz

TRÉMULA.

Búscame entre las
copas de edificios
y los árboles,
entre
el claxon feroz

y el silbido del tamalero.
Búscame y hallarás
el lado escondido del sol.

Flor Aguilera,
Mexico City, Mexico

Croon

The stars, the moon, the sun, the sea, the sand—
enough for every poet in the land
to hang a heart upon and pluck life's strings
with lonesome, longing, lingering lover's hand.

The sand, the sea, the moon, the sun, the stars
belong to us alone, jam-packed in jars
of words to open as a heady balm:
a poultice for our precious secret scars.

The sun, the sand, the sea, the stars, the moon,
and everything between from spoon to swoon
will fill this interstice, our darling space
where frailty's bliss is grace, a sweet monsoon.

The sea, the stars, the sand, the moon, the sun…
Clichés galore in measured lines of fun!
A white so bright it burns our patterns black.
Cocaine for rhymesters living on the run.

The moon, the sun, the stars, the sand, the sea:
What more could any wordsmith want to be
or not to be? The question drifts to shore
grows feet in time and waltzes metrically.

Felicia Sanzari Chernesky,
Flemington, New Jersey USA

青春十六天

李颖妍；内蒙古自治区呼和浩特市新城区

倘若我描述青春

那么一朵花可以发言

太阳借作花托 月亮拼凑成花瓣 星星碾为花蕊

茂盛为小半个宇宙

热烈明媚的底色 撑起

或满或缺绽放 晦涩与凝重蜿蜒行走出纹路

总有深邃的想象与希冀

是昼夜交替的天空

探索 星星钻磨出无数个洞

求知 咬出月牙状的味道

义无反顾 不急不缓 晕染开明暗与刚柔

假如我推迟一天青春死去的行程

到宇宙里 变成十六天

是整个夏天最后的长情

微笑 眼泪 热忱 通通献祭

炼成不朽的墓园

青春在阳光里 在月光里 星光里

Li Yingyan,
Hohhot New District, Inner Mongolia

I'd Like to Trill You a Song About End-Words

I'd like to trill you a song about end-words.
Moon about how many tenses there could be.
Mountain Time knolls to the mouth of eternity.
Nighttime knows to sling its lune in broad light.
Today I'll sweep five sun rinds into my nightie.
Napping all day noons into *mad reclamation of self.*
Anyhow *Moon's* now short for *Onward to Mars.*
On board will be seated a pair of *phantom torsos*—
Helga + Zohar to deck in the lower spacecraft.
Only the latter to wear that cool protective vest.
The word *Zohar* vines from *those who are wise.*
I hereby dub Mme. Zohar my *muse-statuette.*
I'd like to family-farm a new tense—thing is,
Zohar's stoic torso keeps thumping on about zeds.

Diane Raptosh,
Boise, Idaho USA

Sa araw na naging tamis.
Baka ay hindi ako titigil sa pagmamahal sa iyo katulad noong dati.
Sa buwan na naging maasim.
ikaw pa rin at para sa 'yo ang aking braso.
Sa araw at buwan, kayo ang aking inspirasyon.
Sa araw na sa umaga ay aking kasiyahan.
At sa buwan na sa gabi'y aking kasiyahan.
Sana hindi niyo ako iiwan, sana hindi kayo tutulad sa mga bituin.

Jhemar Lagata,
Misamis Occidental, Region X, Philippines

In The Comfort Of Light

As a disaster takes hold
of the world, what is it like

> *When you feel despondent,*

to live a life stalled? What is it
like to yearn for a web of stars,

> *search for a prophetic omen,*

circling the sky, for moonlight
floating overhead: a heavenly

> *sign of hope, an encouraging luster.*

veil of comfort? There is no
better healing for the spirit

> *There is no better cure*

than light's serene reflection
over a river's silvery surface,

> *than sun flooding moon, enlightening*

the flamboyance of waves
soothing as radiant gleams flicker

> *with luminous signs.*

on and off, their jubilant dance:
ethereal. Each evening as soon as

> *A row of candles sparkle and shine.*

starlight taps on walls, I take
a much-needed stroll for the soul.

> *Come with me to the creek*

As the moon and stars speak,
I listen to their harmonious trill,

> *where cardinals flit branch to branch.*

resounding like warblers' songs.
Lost in the wash of light, I let go

> *Release anger. Stroll down paths.*

of darkness, bask in the cuddle
of beams, surrender to night's thrall.

> *Seek comfort in sky's divine radiance.*

> *Carolyn Kreiter-Foronda,*
> *Hardyville, Virginia USA*

Long Light

In memory of Ryan White,

      for Dr. Anthony Fauci

How did we ever survive this long

Stumbling through the dark

Plagues of disease and hate?

By finally following those lonely leaders

Into the long light

Of enlightenment and love.

Matthew Graham,
Evansville, Indiana USA

칠월칠석날/ 채현병

한낮의 빗방울은 상봉의 눈물방울

한밤의 빗방울은 이별의 눈물방울

후두둑 떨어지기 전에 신방부터 차리세

Chae, Hyun-byung,
Siheung-si, Gyeonggi-do, Republic of Korea

The Grandmother Who Fell from the Sky

My grandmother fell from the sky when she was six years old.
The mayflies arrived at the same time, rising in a bright cloud
over the pond. I have the black and white photo to prove it.
She wore a summer dress that day, thin anklets, and shoes
sturdy enough for the journey—a haze of mayflies
forming a crown above her raven hair. She arrived
carrying a kitten. I've often wondered if the kitten
was falling from the sky, too, and she caught
him in her sun-gold arms while in dreamtime.
My grandmother had a crooked smile.
I always thought this was the result of her entering
earth's atmosphere. You know the kind of smile I mean—
the one where one side is higher than the other end,
as if gravity had no power in that sacred opening.
No one really knows her place of origin,
although some in the family would argue she was born
on an August morning to my great-grandparents. Of course,
back then, there were no birth records and none of her siblings
are alive to speak of it. I know she had her own language.
There were times when we were together and she would slip
into another dimension. Mostly times when we walked
among her flowers—her garden an asterism of pentas, star
jasmine, ferns, and moss roses that grew
in the cracks of her sidewalk. She spoke to the flowers
as she would speak to anyone—gently. And I swear,
they would respond, their heads nodding in the wind.
Once, during a new moon, while we lay on our backs
watching the sky turn blue-black, she pointed to the first
star and whispered, *I'll be going back there.*
When she died at the young age of seventy-three,
I dreamed of her ascension back into the sky. I watched
as the heavens reclaimed her body—her streaming hair,
high cheek bones, tiny waist, and racehorse ankles.
I witnessed her smile straightening, made new—as she flew
higher and higher, and higher still.

Jessica D. Thompson,
Evansville, Indiana USA

Stjärna/Jolie Bébé Étoile

Quand le noirceur vient pour moi,
Oh Màni.
Ma peau défait, recouverte d'étoiles.
Mes cendres, mais des miettes de terrine,
émeraude, aux yeux de l'aurore elle-même.
Les pointes des plus grands pins blancs,
inaugureront leur ascension; domicile.

Mes atomes acquis, se sont dispersés sur cette-planète moribond.
La conscience qui reste, mais un écho,
dans les ventricules de ce que je laisse derrière.
Mes descendants, seront-ils les gardiens des choses sacrées.
Gardien modeste et inébranlable de Gaïa?

Ma chère lune des moissons,
avec tes chaudes tentes de pissenlit,
dis moi;
Serai-je célébré comme sang et chagrin enchevêtre,
ou comme fils d'alchimie tellurique?

Pleurez-vous, douce Luna,
pour les choses que nous, les humains consommons,
pas par nécessité, mais par cupidité
Vous fondez-vous dans l'aube,
aspirant à une marée nocturne plus en forme?

Quand les mers montent et descendent par ton caprice,
cher Gealach, est-ce votre nature de pardonner,
le misérable noir que nous portons au fond de lui?

Ai-je réussi à rendre mon âme acceptable,
équitable Stjärna.
Pour la providence parmi le cosmos?

D.C.Houston,
Kincardine, Ontario, Canada

Red Moon, Red Sun

red, red full moon
hugging the night,
hiding in moist mist,
kisses clouds
leaving streaks of scarlet
to remember her by

      while
      in another corner of the heavens

            her cousin, the sun
            sends stunning streaks of scarlet
            streaming through steamy skies

R. Bremner,
Glen Ridge, New Jersey USA

LUNA

A woman is rowing a boat in the dark,
    the waters calm, but deep.

Full moon steady ahead, irresistible
    wake of light, her body bent in pursuit.

With every plunge of the oars—impossible
    splash of stars and she, alone, amid.

Cast off maybe from the bigger boat
    of a life long tied to golden days.

She turns her head often to adjust her course,
    the waters deep, but calm.

There is no doubting the moth-like purity
    of her aim,

unreasonable as it is. For her, no rest
    or she will drift

back to her beginning or even past.
    On another night

the trip might be effortless but then
    or now, as the waves beneath no

waves proclaim: arrival is merely a word
    already moving into the space beyond.

The poem's in the rowing, the ink-dark sea,
    the pull of moonlit arms.

Lynne Burnett,
Parksville, British Columbia, Canada

Earthshine

seen from the moon ...

We regard the slow strafing
of the stars, record their blind sailing
high across the dome of larger dark;
reflect on the reflections of the lights
that drift off past the final spark
to where all prophecy
and measurement collapses.

O world among lost rocky worlds,
reef in the waterless ocean,
provider of the sad account
of how we swallowed everything,
what have we done wrong but eat you?
Blue apple long fallen from the tree
we cannot comprehend,
its branches blanched and stubbled,
its windfall of worlds, stem end over
blossom end, falling one by one
into nothing.

Tom Chandler,
Bristol, Rhode Island USA

Gizhebaa

Omaa Akiing
N giiwitaashimotawaa dewe'igan. ,
Ishpiming nagamowag anangoog.
Ondaasigeng anangong ani noondaagwad.
Gizhibaabizod Giizhig,
Gaa kizhibaashimowaad
Giizis, Dibik Giizis, Anangoog
Awe gaa ozhitood enakiiwangin–
Nanaboozhoo, Mooz, Gaa pibooniked, Misi Bizhiw
Ishpiming anangoog
noojimo'iwewaad zhaabojiwan
giizhigong inaateng
Bagonegiizhig
Jiibay-ziibi
Ojiig'anung
jiibay kana
Giwedin'anung
Mishi bizhiw
Mooz
Maang

Waabanang inaateng mizhakii.
Waabanang Ndasemaake.
Waabanang noondawishin
        Zoongan miinawaa onizhishin
Waabanang Gi boozhoo'in bagosenjigeng
Waabanang bezhig miinawaa giizhigak ndani bimaadiz.
Waabanang Mbagosendaan nibwaakaawin.
        Anangoowininiwag ogete gikendaasowiniwaan
Waabanang ndizhinikaaz. ,
        Nga bimi niimi'aa njichaag
        Imaa sa ishpiming.
        Onabiyaan imaa anangokaang
        Ge gikinoowizhiwaad manidoog
                        Denise Lajimodiere,
                Turtle Mountain Band of Ojibwe

106

Night Artist

Dusk awakens to the impossible palette of an artist's colors
A perishing sun paints the sky in still wet altered hues.
Crimson reds, fiery opaque orange bursts, entwined with gold.
Through my glass window a small rectangular block of sky is framed
Frozen breathless, confined in a room.

The evening kaleidoscope unfolds-

Grey cloud curtains open slowly
Across the artificial screen of wonder
Darkness with desolate, infinite beauty
Driving the sun from view.
Feelings of guilt, for I have lived a sinful and ordinary life.

The artist paints a crescent moon and a new illumination gives birth-

Two cosmic planets
Lovingly anchored with threads of broken stars
One heavier than the other pulls the moon to a final resting place
The crescent, unnatural and disproportionate smiles that all is forgiven
The brushstroke of God is complete.

Carl Scharwath,
New Smyrna Beach, Florida USA

化为星辰：为祁红而作

每次想你

　　　　无不有一个光点闪现

　所以在整个夜晚

你都有漫天的星光照亮前程

就像

每次想你

无不有一个花蕾绽开

　　所以你每到一处

　都有鲜花簇拥着你

与太阳同行：为祁红而作

　　　每当我在地球的这一边

起身下床去迎接朝霞之时，而你那边

却正值你上床就寝

或者，每当你在太平洋的彼岸

起身拥抱初升的太阳之际，而我

却在这边的暮色中渐渐迷失了自己。

　　　　　　生活在

　　　对面

不同的时区，我们为彼此守着岁：

我仿若你的影子追随你渡过白天

或似你昨夜留下的真实碎片

而你总是在地球那边严防着黑暗

入侵我白日的梦幻

　都是为了确保我们俩

　即使在午夜也有充足的阳光

月光之下：为祁红而作

从我心中、还有你的

心源，我们之间的爱也许从不深沉

但它会持续不停地流淌

是的，就像源头远在伊甸园的小溪

穿过无数的灌木和鹅卵石

　　　在昼夜之间

　　　　纯净而清澈

它会不顾地球上所有的延误和弯路

仿佛在所有气泡都蒸发而

　　　　化入月光之后

一直要向前

　　　流入大海

Changming Yuan,
Vancouver, Canada

108

Dear Editor

Stars, Sun or Moon must appear
in these lines to qualify the enterprise
to be suited and tucked in to a box
to be sent to the Southern pole of
the Moon. I wonder why Earth,
or any living or dead thing in the
still blue planet cannot instead
provide the subject. Surely, aliens
who may discover the capsule would
be curious about the place of origin,
its human and earthly inspiration.
But I reside in North America,
hence my task. Perhaps, scribes
from other regions will carry
the fire and the water, so to speak,
so we offer a complete picture
of the planet's poetry except for
speech signals the human ear
cannot hear, that dolphins and
whales emit, or casting our eyes
above on geese, half their brains
asleep while flying in formation,
we can note these and all other
marvels to furnish our stanzas
that Earth offers. But not everything
can serve as subject of every verse,
so for richer or poorer, in sickness
and for the health of the lyric,
and for this particular trip
I offer you here Sun, Moon and all
the Stars in the sky of this poem.

Indran Amirthanayaz,
Rockville, Maryland USA

Depuis l'espace

Poussière d'étoiles
sous les paupières
soleils roses, soleils sombres
pour la danse
des jours et des nuits
et le cœur qui s'affole
comme lors d'un vertige
où chaque pas
risque
de nous faire chuter.

Vue depuis l'espace, la Terre
nous effraie
avec son visage de clown
défiguré
et sa lune
à la merci
de toutes les illusions.

Louise Dupré,
Montréal, (Québec) Canada

遥远的星光

我不在乎这次离别

即使星光那样的遥远

可是握手道别的夜晚

我的心有些震颤

一语道不破

只淡淡的说声再见

让这舒朗的月光

印在你的脑海

留在我的心际

有朝一日忆起今晚

生活的路会坦荡如砥

Liu jie,
Zhoukou City, China

Crescent witness

On a desolate ground in Kyiv
This spring, the
Moon landed on a
Ravaged window sill
Its
Frayed edges of
Hope breaking out in dark spots

At the assault, its cover blown.

The flames from a thousand guns
Erupted in a place not far away
Lighting the devastation,
Advancing in ominous steps,
The moon held its breath
Mute witness,
Shifting ground.

Inside, there were remnants of
Upturned beds, broken toys
Limbs,
The things that constitute disaster
And the only placebo

For miles and miles
Was a crescent
Hanging on for dear life
On a broken window sill

Soft gentle glow
Of sadness
Remembering better days,
Better things.

Smeetha Bhoumik,
Mumbai, India

加油,武汉!

天空在哭泣，巨浪在侵袭。

没有人知道，没有人知道它何时会停止。

汹涌的波涛穿透一切。

鸟类失去庇护所，变得无家可归。

老年人淹死;年轻的呻吟。

没有人知道，没有人知道它何时会停止。

慢性瘟疫使朽烂的遗体

简陋的住所和匮乏的食物。

受伤的鸟儿就像野兽一样

没完没了地打滚。

然而，

勇敢的医生投身于汹涌的巨浪中

征服和利用。

雏鸟

不情愿地被送往安全的地方

冷冰冰的眼泪。

Zhao Zichen,
Zhoukou City, Henan Province, China

Stars, moons, suns, "We are humans, Earthians, do you know us?"

i.
Of dirt. Soil. Humans are more grounded than they believe. Do you know us?

ii.
Earthians, of terrain beneath. From the core, did we rise? Do you know us?

iii.
Or placed on land, that of Earth, by hands unfamiliar? Do you know us?

iv.
Or coupling seeds, atoms, sculpting mud from our bodies. Do you know us?

v.
Stars glow in, around us. Lights flash, souls flutter. Beings. Do you know us?

vi.
Moons come and go. Time rises, sleeps. Time lifts, destroys. Do you know us?

vii.
How many Suns are out there? In blank space? Gifting life? Do you know us?

viii.
Some say genes are real. Biology divides. Do you know us?

xi.
Some avowed, used genes to split, hate, control, rule. Do you know us?

x.
Skin, hair, body, declared ugly-different by some. Do you know us?

xi.
It's what some have, others don't. Luck, destiny it is. Do you know us?

xii.
Some are like, "aint ever gonna be a rainy day". Do you know us?

xiii.
Some alchemists keep chipping, refining, recreating. Do you know us?

xiv.
Human, man, woman, LGBTQ, children, multitudes in one. Do you know us?

xv.
Movies, conspiracies hammer… you are watching us. Do you know us?

xvi.
Some say, experimenting on us. Kidnapping us. Do you know us?

xvii.
Come in peace. We just seek to know, we aren't alone. Do you know us?

xviii.
We aint best cosmic children. Constant learners, churners. Do you know us?

xxi.
Cocktails of tides, flares, air, stars, moon, sun, spirits. Do you know us?

xx.
Do you know us? We of you? You of us? Are you there? Do you know us?

Anita Nahal,
Jersey City, New Jersey USA

Astronomy "In Perfect Silence"

A million-petalled flower of being there, Seattle,
     beside Bagley Hall in a time long ago,
   can you see the magic in the water,
     Drumheller Fountain, Lake Washington, Mt. Rainier
   even as students rush inside to class? Never
forget what enthusiasm for a subject can do:

gone the professor's name but not these lessons--
     how Intro to Astronomy never left me.
   Important to look up at the stars, each day,
     just to remember our insignificance. All term,
   know that we're mere specks. Keep reading,
learning about blue dwarfs, red giants, binary stars, our silver

moon and other celestial bodies, constellations, comets,
     nebulae, all the ways scientists study
   our universe from a distance. Where is earth's
     place if everything's streaming away?
   Quasars and quarks—these aren't the only
rich mysteries. There's more. Dark matter, black holes,

serious topics still to be figured out. In the book, star charts,
     timely as always. I step out with one, frigid January,
   under a brilliant sky. Auriga, Capella, Pleiades, and there's
     Venus rising. A skyscape admired each time.
   Walt Whitman was right: somehow to balance
excitement with knowledge. Seeing night skies again:

     yearly, monthly, daily—gazing overhead, still awed,
zealous, "I look'd up in perfect silence at the stars."

Patricia Clark,
Grand Rapids, Michigan USA

La víspera

Préstame, Luna, tu redonda cara

de niña campesina que, en espera

del festival, se prende lentejuelas

y luce su careta de hojalata;

préstame tu mirar y tu gozoza

sonrisa relumbrante,

que viene mi amante!

Sol que maduras de maíz el oro,

la dulce caña, y de la berenjena

el soberbio color; tú que dominas

desde el cielo la siembra y la cosecha,

ayúdame a cocer—que sepa a besos!—

manjar que delirante

le serviré a mi amante!

Y ustedes que en lo oscuro de la noche

todo lo ven, descubren y tantean—

alerta tribu de estrellas, cuyas luces

jamás se apagan aunque no se vean,

iluminen con recelo y sin cesar

todo el camino por donde jadeante

viene mi amante!

Rhina P. Espaillat,
Newburyport, Massachusetts USA

117

Pesanan Muktamad

Dari Mentari. Purnama. Kejora.

Sejak azali, dunia ini berpaksi. Menjadi saksi
pada segala yang berlaku di langit, di ufuk.
Indahnya alam semesta, dari pelangi tujuh
warna hingga ke bintang bertaburan
membentuk buruj. Manusia mengagumi
segala keagungan.

Sinar mentari silih berganti
Angin samudera menolak awan
Masa tidak mengenal mati
Dunia berubah mengikut zaman

Masa berlalu, dunia terus berputar. Menjadi
saksi pada keindahan di daratan, di lautan.
Indahnya alam semesta, dari belantara tujuh
benua hingga ke samudera tiada
bersempadan. Manusia impikan segala
keagungan.

Purnama setia terus menyinar
Tersembunyi bintang di langit
Manusia leka masih tak sedar
Dunia didera teramat sakit

Akhir zaman, dunia terlalu sibuk. Menjadi
saksi pada kemusnahan di sungai, di gunung.
Alam semesta memberontak, dari tujuh bah
besar yang melanda hingga bencana puting
beliung. Manusia masih tamakkan
keagungan.

Kejora tidak dapat menolong
Menangis pun apa kan daya
Angan-angan tinggi melambung
Kita masih boleh mengejar masa

Adakah masa lagi? Kita cuma mampu
berharap.

Apakah warisan untuk anak cucu Adam?
Manusia kian kacau bilau, dari khalifah
hingga ke ummah pelbagai ragam. Dari
saintis hingga ke perintis penuh berakal.
Yang kaya raya dan juga yang papa kedana,
mencari harta. Kini, cuma tinggal harapan
dan doa.

Manusia merindui segala keagungan.

Ninot Aziz,
Malaysia

To the Beauty and the Mystery at Surge Narrows

To the great spirit rainforest holding up half the sky, the sun and the moon in its arms, whose rings drink the collective memories of a time before diesel fuel, before the rusted propane tank petrified by the slow accretions of sand and moss and tree roots – now a strange artifact to the banality of the Anthropocene. To the raw earth that smells of wet straw and the placenta of a newborn faun, that crumbles between fingers, cool on the tips, gooey like bread dough in the palm, pulsing with life; and the way the sea air inflates lungs without effort, brings joy to the restless without sound but the timpani of a live, beating heart.

> A heart born of sun –
> the multifoliate star
> blooms anew in fire!

To the waters surging past like absolution. To the kelp covered driftwood circling back to the shore, an echo of the questions posed by the Sufi poet, as though the world had tilted a little to pour out a wonder too big to fully comprehend it without surrendering to the miraculous. To the fog lifting above small islets, before swallowing them again when cloud and sea birth a wild garden of rose at sunset, the yellow sturgeon moon; to show there is more we cannot see in this world than is revealed in every moment of our desperate lives.

> Passages of black water
> writ in scattered reflections from sunset –

To the slap of a whale's fin just beyond sight that announces your arrival, saying, again and again, *you are home, you belong here*; but the water is cold, as cold as truth, too cold to swim out as fish, become Jonah seeking salvation in that galaxy of a million tiny stars formed from rotating gases as deep as a whale's stomach. To the sea otter, who watches with coral eyes, playful as a puppy in the shallows at the back of the cove, who welcomes your spirit like the child away for a month with nothing to give but admiration.

> Oh, still moon! Fireflies!
> Guide the weary traveller
> through that grove of stars.

To the red fox standing on a log beneath pillars of ancient fir, a prophet with wisdom at the tip of his whiskers larger than the philosophies of sea and rain, melting into the undergrowth like a sacred ghost, but not before pronouncing, *here, this is your life, live it*. To each humble slug on the path hewed by pilgrims, hemmed by ferns up to the waist, that seem to be everywhere all at once, who demands we look long enough to behold the beauty in even the smallest of things.

> Tiny butterfly,
> tiny spark of life becomes
> the soul of being.

Rob Omura,
Calgary,Alberta, Canada

Saludo cósmico

Si pudiera adivinar a qué sol,
estrella, galaxia o habitante
mi poesía apuntara.

Si al menos una partícula galáctica
depositara luz en mi oscuridad diaria.
Pero todo se reduce al deseo,
escandalosa visión de un firmamento arcano.

Lo que ofrezco es el verbo
nacido del limo terrestre y visceral,
placer o agonía, torpe vocablo.
Poco parece, pero algo es.

No entiendo el universo, ni él parece
entenderme a mí.
Mi ignorancia es preclara.
Por eso me limito a contemplar su azul
que aquí, en mis montañas,
se percibe impoluto y transparente,
sueño, esfinge, esquirla de estrella sideral.

Intuyo lo que no alcanzan mis mermados ojos,
autopistas celestes, altares impregnados de silencio,
flores que son estrellas o al menos asemejan
allí en lo alto y profundo, donde no hay norte ni sur,
señales en las esquinas o parámetros
para la orientación.

Allí va este poema sin destinatario, propósito o tema.
Es un saludo poético, la tinta de la aurora,
lo más modesto de nuestro universo cultural.
Lo que se dice sin decir y apenas sugiere.
El primer signo de nuestro pedestre universo.

Fernando Operé,
Madrid, Spain

MARE FRIGORIS

Coming home late spring night, stars a foreign
Language above me, I thought I would know

The moon like family, its dark plains -- sea of
Crises, sea of nectar, serpent sea.

How quickly a century passes,
Minerals crystallize at different speeds,

Limestone dissolves, rivers sneak through its absence.
This morning I learned painted turtles

Sleeping inches below the streambank
Freeze and do not die. Fifteen degrees

Mare Frigoris, sea of cold, second
Quadrant of the moon's face. I slide toward

The cabin, arms full of brown bags, one light
Syrups over drifts of snow. Night rubs

Icy skin against me and I warm
Small delicates -- cilantro, primrose--

Close to my body. A hundred million
Impulses race three hundred miles an hour

Through seventeen square feet of skin and
Gravity that collapses stars, lifts earth's

Watery dress from her body, holds me

With such tenderness I hardly breathe.

Sandra Alcosser,
Florence, Montana, USA

Mar de estrellas

Joyas multicolor del firmamento
acompañan mi soledad nocturna
ellas me cuentan miles de historias
en esta oscuridad profunda.

Conforme transcurren
las horas líquidas
las nubes llegan con luces
parpadeantes de tormenta
y la luna se esconde
tras su velo de algodón.

Ahora el sonido del trueno
llena todo a su alrededor
con el sonido de su voz
ensordecedora.

Tiempo y corazón se congelan
al compás de los miles
de cristales líquidos
que envuelven la eternidad.

Eugenia Nájera Verástegui,
Tampico, Tamaulipas, México

Arms Full of Apricots

Quick come see!

The night heavens have pulled

Back their drapery

And all the stars are showing themselves.

There is a bear out there. He is

Dancing before the mountain El Salto.

Ecstatic, arms full of apricots,

He is abandoning himself to the moon.

Ruthelen Burns,
Arroyo Seco, New Mexico USA

朗照的月

没有风的夜晚

会有目光撩起你的发

我平静的手像夜

涂抹你的肌**肤**

你在和谐的曲线中

移向朗月

我自心的高度窥视

你眼光的味道

爱 静止地穿过孤独

恋人在红宝石的寂寞中 等待

而倾斜向东方的残月

美丽的

让人不敢对视着喘息

那残月

如此地照耀两颗斑驳的心

那残月

如此地照耀一千次回眸

不是朗朗的白

而是泛着桔色红的微笑

如你的脸庞

126

转向我一万次的热吻

胜过所有恋人等待的心情

今夜 沉思的我陷入夜

漂移的圆尚还没有佳期

你在哪里朗照我的幽梦？

Su Hao
Shanghai City, China

A LAKE WITH GEESE FLYING OVER

"All things are one thing and that one thing is all things."

--John Steinbeck

One bead of dew on a single feather
of a single goose is the whole flock,
is all birds everywhere; one wave
turning white, then curling under,
then gone, is all waves of the lake,
is all water everywhere; one bead
of dew, one white wave tip is
the Earth; is the moon, is the stars,
is the cosmos.

David Evans,
Soiux Falls, South Dakota USA

Loose At Midnight

The moon goes hollow in the night,
A hole to pass through,
As ends of stars lie over our bed and my eyelids,
Over stones in pastures,
Grandfolk under graveyards of grass, an outlier's skull
Sunk in a mound,
The bones of a horse, bleached in an all-out gallop on a
Hillside--

I turn to you, then turn the knob and turn to the sky
And next to Orion the stars are startled to see this
Black horse emerge through the moon's dark half,
Flanks flecked with saliva and flying foam,
And turn to seize again its hillside slant,
Turning to your dream-drenched truth.

Larry Woiwode,
Jamestown, North Dakota USA

The Polaris Trilogy 3

Ice,
Wind,
Fire

Ice

Thirteen Ways of Looking At Antarctic Ice

I
In the shadow of the nunataks
The only thing moving
Is snow blowing across ice.

II
The only sounds are snow
Hitting flapping tent walls,
And the popping and cracking of ice
As it moves glacially below.

III
The blowing snow whirls
In the katabatic winds
Making drifts on the ice.

IV
The drifts, over time,
Harden into solid structures.
"Sastrugi" that look like breaching dolphins
Or frozen, foamy, waves of snow.

V
I do not know which to prefer,
The beauty of the blowing snow,
Or the beauty of the shapes
It leaves in its wake.

VI
Icicles only form
On beards, moustaches, and hair.
Frozen breath
Creating more ice from within.
The mood precarious,
Knowing safe outdoor time is limited.

VII
Machines move us
Across the snow,
Rhythmic bobbing
Up and down on frozen waves.

VIII
When a dark black dot
Comes into view
The cold melts away.
Excitement replaces discomfort.

IX
At the sight of the meteorite
Sitting on blue ice
Even the most stoic
Smile with delight.

X
To be the first to see
A piece of outer space
A piece of another planetary body,
To recover it
Before the ice swallows it for centuries,
Is exhilarating.

XI
Collecting the rocks
to take back to the lab
to learn where, when, and how
it, and we, come from.

XII
The river of ice is moving,
Taking undiscovered black rocks with it.

XIII
The evening sun
(for it rarely snows)
Shines on those rocks
Recovered
As they sit in a box
in the glistening ice
Waiting to reveal their secrets.

Catherine Corrigan,
Antarctica

0.

Hoy
la medianoche
es un muro

                                           de hielo.

Su frío
se siente como una máquina,
como un recuerdo
como un muro,
y con ese tono pinta toda la existencia,
se ríe de nosotros,
 mira nuestros defectos
 y juega todo
 a lo seguro:
La Blanca Inocencia.

El hielo espera
es su virtud,
abraza estas arenas del tiempo
cuando los hijos
se vuelven fuego en la memoria,
un sacrificio.

Pero este mar de hielo puede más,
se mete en la pared
gana terreno en la cama,
Y cuando,
La medianoche y yo nos miramos,
hay nieve derretida en cada pregunta que se calla
en sus respuestas oscuras,
y en mis remedos de luz.

                             Hoy
                       la medianoche
                         es un mar

de hielo.

                           Luis Alonso Cruz Alvarez,
                                Lima, Perú

Daughter / Father

A very drunk drunk weaves along footpath
winding through a park that mocks Eden.
Firewater, high noon, ghost moon.

From opposite direction,
at footpath intersection, lightly
pirouettes an icy ballerina.

Just audible Slap! backhand / cheek.
Never knew what hit him but
it was not accidental.

Branch? Bird? Memory?
She spins, spins and spins
towards some loftier oblivion.

Allan Lake,
Victoria, Australia

Ice at the South Pole
Vastly visible on Earth
hiding on The Moon

Ben Bussey,
Antarctica

Wind

Love in a time of chaos, a cento
After James Joyce

I hear an army charging upon the land,
thunder of horses plunging, foam about their knees:
arrogant, in black armour, the charioteers come out of the sea,
run shouting by the shore their battle-name: clanging, clanging
upon the heart as upon an anvil.

Earth and heaven tremble, vast wings above the lambent waters
brood—
a waste of water sways, uplifts its weedy mane, and the dark rain
falling,
wind whines and whines the shingle, each single slimesilvered
stone.
As the twilight turns, the lamp fills with a pale green glow:
a birdless heaven, seadusk, one lone star piercing the west,
paler than time's wan wave—the voice of winter at the door.
Sing about the long deep sleep, leave dreams to the dreamers:
the time of dreaming, dreams is over.

Desolate winds assail with cries the shadowy garden where love is,
the moon a web of silence in this witchery.
Sad as the sea-bird going forth alone,
the winds cry to the water's monotone,
the grey winds are blowing where I go.

When over us the wild winds blow, lightly come or lightly go
at the hour of evenstar as ghostfires from heaven's far
arch on night's sindark nave, the trysting and the twining star—
all night a veil, for love at first is all afraid.
Hurry over the dark lands and run upon the sea
for seas and lands shall not divide us
you, my love and me.

Come, blind me with your kiss, bend deeper on me,
take me, save me at that hour when all things have repose.
Eastward the gradual dawn prevails—tremble all those veils:

do you hear the night wind sigh
at that hour when soft lights
come and go in the air above
and in the earth below.

This poem is constructed entirely of line fragments from poems by James Joyce.

Anne Casey,
Northbridge, Australia

Cold catabatics

bring frostnip through paintball mask

while hunting space rocks.

Rob Coker,
Antarctica

Voyage to Katherine via Andromeda

Over Catfish waterhole, oyster-tinted clouds foreshadow rain. Desert ladies rest in dogwood shade, after Sunday's hunt—still wearing their Jesus T-shirts after church. Late light threaded with goanna smoke and rays. The sun folds tangerine across the shallows, where my dog Moon thrashes, seal-white, through algae-darkened reeds. It's King Brown territory, but the snakes have been quiet lately. And I tell myself it's just exhaustion—how he trembles, how he drags himself weakly up the bank. But by the time I've reached him, Moon is foaming at the mouth. Night already drumming in the Red River Gums. The old ladies can't find the bite, but we know. We know—and there's no antivenom for 700 kilometres, not even for people. On the phone, the vet in Katherine is blunt and kind. Five hours past snakebite, she says, the convulsions end and he'll go into cardiac arrest. If his heart holds out, antivenom might save him. But most dogs don't make it. Most are dead by Top Springs. No one drives in the Tanami desert after dark, when dry storms rearrange the dunes, when night-coloured bison stand like caryatids in the road. I borrow a friend's Toyota, Moon lying rigid across my lap, his teeth bared—and I drive, not slowing, not stopping, just driving and driving until dawn or he dies. We pass into that blackness like a needle. Mount Herbert appears in blue lightning, then darkness swallows the trees.

Monsoon makes the desert electric. Floodwaters pool, horizon to horizon, under bands of solemn stars. Deep space is a globe curving above and below—galaxies, the drifting nebulae, satellites reflecting in the water's beetle-black. We travel between mirrored worlds like an orbiting craft, like venom racing toward the heart. Over sounds of engine and thunder and fear, gales erupting from flooded ground, a woman is screaming into the desert—screaming, please, please, don't fucking take my dog. And for a moment, the wind drops. There's a calm that comes when everything is finished. I pull myself together and for the next six hours, just talk to him—inventing stories of miraculous dogs with bodies of lightning and serpents and rain. I tell him what he means to me. I tell him he's a good dog—winding my voice out like a rope to hold him, to stop him unravelling into that whirring spinning night. Near Mount Glass, we swerve around a python stretched across the road, its slow head lifting to taste the storm. There's a tailwind coming in from the bombing ranges, carrying radioactive dust. The owls feel it, as they blade through cooler currents, away from the speeding car. An omen feather holds a moment against the windscreen, then the air takes it. And rushing beside the car, night fills with blinding forms—the familiar ghosts and others: Robyn, silvered by headlights, in her floating hospital gown. Alfy with his belt wound tightly around his throat. He tumbles across the bonnet, then out into the bush.

We reach Top Springs five hours after snakebite—Moon deathly still. If he goes into cardiac arrest, I'll stop driving, just be with him until it's over, until he passes where I can't follow. I hold my palm against his snout for proof of life and find the rhythm of his breath.   50 kilometres out of Katherine there's a car on fire—violently beautiful. Embers lift from its fenders like miniature suns, like flecks in a burning lizard's eye. I pull over but no one's in sight—just another stolen car, and there's no time left. A door in the sky has opened and travellers pass in both directions. We lose the back end of the Toyota, skidding into Katherine at 2am. A police car does a U-Turn to follow, peeling away outside the animal hospital. Older snakes, the vet says, conserve their venom. She says he was lucky, gives him antivenom and fluids. She says it was a warning.   It's still dark. Birds congregate silently on the supermarket roof. Not a breath of wind. A barely visible aurora is spreading on the low Eastern rim, eclipsing Perseus and the pointer stars in Centaurus. We're waiting, as I know some of you do too, when the night seems endless—waiting for those birds to open their beaks, for the madrigals of firetails and corellas, butcherbirds, magpies and wrens . . . for the lion sun to wake and walk among the palms, igniting their fans a brilliant night-parrot green. From the Toyota's roof, we watch dawn cross the empty shopping mall carpark. Moon, wrapped in bulldust, leans against my arm—solid and planetary, impossibly alive.

Judith Nangala Crispin
Wamboin NSW, Australia

137

Carried on the Wind

Sounds carry on the wind,
        carry in the wind,
                sometimes are the wind,
                        deafening the soul.
Sand carries on the wind,
        in the wind
                and sometimes is the wind,
                        stripping the paint.
Tears carry on the wind,
        in the wind
                and sometimes are the wind,
                        spreading desert rain.
Hope carries on the wind,
        in the wind,
                and sometimes is the wind
                        of whispered prayers.
Tomorrow carries on the wind,
        in the wind
                and sometimes is the wind
                        of soaring birds.
Writing carries on the wind,
        in the wind
                and sometimes is the wind

                of Heaven.

Doug Jacquier,
Yankalilla, Australia

The burning cold wind

A promise in the barren

A stone from beyond

Wyatt Fries,
Antarctica

Windy Antarctic

Draws you in sweeps you away

You belong there now

Marc Fries,
Antarctica

Fire

Breve historia del fuego

Juan carga un montón de leña para encender la hoguera de San Juan.
Juan desbroza el maíz seco, la chala que envolvió las mazorcas que fueron alimento.
Juan corta las ramas y las flores de suncho que se encienden y apagan, veloces y ruidosas, como la vida misma.
Juan arruga páginas de periódicos entre la leña, importantes noticias que ya nada importan, historia que pronto será fina ceniza.
El nieto de Juan lo ve, expectante, en su afán de preparar el fuego.
El abuelo y el niño encienden estrellas de artificio en la tiniebla.
El niño escribe el nombre del abuelo –Juan– con las estrellas.
El abuelo mira el fuego con ese mismo asombro antiguo de todos los hombres y todas las mujeres desde que supieron atrapar el rayo.
El niño salta –es tradición– sobre las dos hogueras de la huerta.
Los perros ladran, la luna brilla sobre las fogatas como en el título de Pavese.
Año tras año la luna mira impertérrita –si es que mira– envejecer al abuelo.
Juan sabe que ya no tiene las fuerzas de antes para cargar la leña, cortar el maíz seco y las flores de suncho, trasladar pilas de papel periódico hasta el lugar de la fogata.
El niño ignora que Juan se consume como un leño, que él mismo crece entre fogata y fogata, que sus ojos de asombro se cubren con ceniza y los ojos del abuelo con la niebla.
Ahora el nieto carga los montones de leña. La chala y el suncho.
El abuelo, cansado, lo ve en su afán de preparar el fuego cada junio.
Un San Juan cualquiera, el nieto está solo ante cenizas frías.
Otro San Juan cualquiera, el nieto se ha hecho padre y decide volver a encender fuego con sus hijos en el campo, lejos de la ciudad donde ya no es posible encender nada.
Mientras apila leña, les habla del abuelo con palabras que son ramas, que son maíz, que son flores, que son alimento.
Se abre en su pecho, como un rescoldo, el antiguo asombro que Juan sabía despert entre las huertas.
Descubre que el viento se lleva las cenizas, que sigue siendo un niño, que el abuelo ahora escribe su nombre entre los astros.
Enciende el fuego. De nuevo el niño salta sobre las hogueras.

Gabriel Chávez Casazola,
Santa Cruz de la Sierra, Bolivia

Fire

All winter, the Illawarra sun
surfed behind the dark wave of Mt Keira.
Our campfire split pedals open to a Golden Lotus.
We stoked and spat stories in the snip-snaps.
Flickering flames kindled like lambs
popping hot ambered faces from the frozen past.
My eyes spiral the swirling ember seeds
sending our starry minds high into nights
ancient pot where our tales nest and twinkle,
then, re-enter retellings on phoenix wings.

Then came summer when the sun gasped
behind masks of a scorched mountain dune.
A thick haze of wordless Flying Foxes,
feathered charred pages from an unread Earth.
We turned our backs to the abattoirs to
face an uncontained *symmetry of fear*.
Nature screams at our tortured tiger-hold.
As power roars and puffs down our home,
all that remains are silent fireplaces,
standing like gravestones on graved ash.

John Kennedy,
West Wollongong, Australia

Corazón de fuego

Apareció una vez más, durante un viaje, ellos dijeron, era fuego
Ella nacerá, nadie lo sabía, su espíritu de niña como si fuera fuego

La mejor sonrisa combinaba con sus ojos pícaros
Un solitario espíritu, guiando, corriendo, pensando, pareciera fuego

Es como la fiebre cuando quema, ella siempre decía
Dubitando acerca de qué está pasando por dentro, una mujer libera fuego

Candelabros situados en la habitación, una vez ella leyó
¿Eso logrará derretir nuestros corazones? no hubiera fuego

Te sientes separada del mundo, ella depende de su madre
Llorando a través de la ventana, ella apagó el fantasma que considera fuego

Yo traigo mi mano más cerca de tu corazón, la sabiduría del destino
Hasta el sol lentamente brillará, como primavera fuego

Los cielos romperán en rayos de oro, levántate María
Rico tiempo de otoño, lo que él te hace sentir, es un sueño que exigiera fuego.

Maria Alejandra Fumaroni,
Buenos Aires, Argentina

FUEGO Y PASIÓN

El sabor de tu piel
se impregna en cada poro
aceleras todo mi ser
y enciendes todos mis volcanes.

Quiero despojarte de tus vestidos
morder cada rincón
para que te estremezcas
y sentir cómo hierves por dentro.

Mis manos solo buscan recorrerte
quiero surcar tus límites
perderme donde termina tu universo
besarte en tus profundidades.

Mi pecho sobre tu espalda
nuestras partes se acoplan
tu néctar fluye y solo quiero beberlo
sentir que me nutre y quema.

Respirar tu exhalación
cuando tu cuerpo se pone helado
cuando te estremeces
y me pides que fluya en ti.

Eres toda mi pasión
el rocío que anhelo tomar
el frío que recorre mi espalda
mi fuego de vida.

Cada llama, cada latido
quiero romper todas tus fronteras.
Tú, el manjar más sublime
de esta y todas mis realidades.

Jorge William Tigrero Vaca,
Guayaquil, Ecuador

Together On Earth

Iceberg pillows & an avalanche of satin sheets

I reach for your hand and grasp the arctic abyss.
You greet me with a freezing pat,
sending chills through my back.
My sweat, now snowflakes accompany me
in the absence of your embrace.

We have woven a divergent track,
skating on thin ice, walking on eggshells.
One wrong word or move
and this delicate layer cracks.
Focus on the cracks to watch the suspenseful split.

Let us gather ice & avoid the avalanche
from the hasty hellos & generic goodbyes
and warm it up to heartfelt hellos & graceful goodbyes.
If we add some
honey, we could have it all.

Sleepless, both tossing and turning
but nothing breaks the ice.
The pillow separating us, the tip of the iceberg.
We are afraid to move it and realize what hides underneath
and its unbearable weight.

Our white and glossy pillowcase,
from our wedding night,
a reminder that every frigid night,
we coexist with
arctic foxes, hares and wolves.

If we rewind
we can make our flame reignite.
Soft, satin sheets
you wrap yourself in like a chrysalis
protecting yourself from the Winter.
Steamy, satin sheets we will not need when
we show each other our newly found wings

forged in fire and set to flight
by the mist of the past icy blast
and the desire to bring back Summer in full bloom.

Mariana Orrego Serna,
Colombia

Wind devours ice

Stellar stowaways revealed

First Lunar migrant

Linda Welzenbach,
Antarctica

Safe Words

I don't want safe words
trimmed to comfort
cut down to size
anaesthetised
palatable words
easy on the ear
easy on the eye

I don't want safe words
hemmed in by lies
words on ice
desiccated
dehydrated
rain-checked waiting on
~~call collect~~   compromise

I don't want words
that toe the line or
back away from   knife-sharp edge
words that hide
words that curl and crawl and beg
I don't want your   safe words

I don't want coddling
words that coo
caress away the curious
assuage the furious
placate the dubious
silver tongued promises of   sufficiency
homogenous comfortability
upholding the status quo

I don't want words that
reign me in   suffocated
subjugated
adulterated
devoid of fire

gas lighted
forced to smile
I don't want that kind of   safety

I don't want words
that bluster in
steal my wind
describe my perimeters
prescribe my limiters
simply because you said
it must be so   your words

                    not mine

Claire Bridge,
Victoria, Australia

Waves of wind-carved ground

Ice, volcanic ash, or clay?

Is this Mars or Earth?

Jani Radebaugh,
Antarctica

WARM PRIVATE PLACES

I Marie Betsy Rasmussen
At the end of the world
surrounded by men and baleen
you keep to the captain's cabin
head down and hands clean
while they boil blubber
bleached skeletons in a red caldera
whales and land and sea
claimed by the first
the bold
the bloody

II Silvia Morella de Palma
Flown, swollen and uncomfortable
to a barren base
gentle white slopes faint in moonlight
broken by red buildings
in exact square formation
you are spilled on the bed as
the captain–your husband–
raises a toast to his son
the first born of this place
furthering their claim on virgin land
as you lay spent and cold

III Anonymous
On the frontier, this astounding continent
no one can hear what he calls you
your work vs your word
vs your whore mouth what did you expect out here
this is still cowboy country
and if you don't like it
quit your research and take the next ship out
guess women just aren't tough enough
for hostile environments

IV Felicity Ashton

Two months on the ice
the first woman to cross solo, the first by muscle alone
your strong legs pull sledges
dragging their doubts
an unmapped path over glaciers and proud mountains
left as you discovered it
footsteps fade to snow
but not forgotten

Alex Bassett,
Norwood SA, Australia

THE BALLAD OF METEORITE JOHN

Way way far south where sheets of ice shrink mountains into molehills,
where the toughest folk that ever were will tremble at the windchills,
where sunshine never seems to warm 'cause Summer's just bright Winter,
where showing off your face is dumb 'cause then your nose will splinter,
where you and I, we normal folk, if housed in yellow teepees, would hold it
in so very long we'd prob'ly burst our peepees,
there was a man, a quiet man, by the name of Meteorite John,
who searched that ice for bits of sky that fell down there upon.

Two score and more the years went by, and as those decades finished,
the joys of smaller meteorites had started to diminish.
"They're too damned small" he said with angst,
 "to be of any use! I'm tired of them things so small
there's nothing there to lose!"
And soon the needs of scientists in John's mind paled and faded;
his outlook towards the specimens became completely jaded.
He motioned toward a chondrite, basket-sized and partly weathered ,
and said "this one will grace my home, and keep my dear dog tethered."

"And that one over there," he cried." is just the perfect size,
to hold down all my papers, as you probably surmised,"
 "And this small one, fully rounded, will look dandy on my hat,
and that shiny carbonaceous is a nice toy for my cat,"
"That one down there beside the flag would make a dandy tie-pin,"
"and that howardite will be a plate where my bananas ripen,"
"And cufflinks, I need cufflinks!" he said holding up a pair,
"They are a little heavy but they add a certain flair,
And this one here, with lonsdaleite, I'll have set in my tooth,"
"And this larger one I'll send away to please my sister Ruth"
"And this tiny one, a little gem will dangle from my ear,"
"While this shiny one a ring will make to flash when nerds come near,"
"but what I need, I truly need," he said with arms spread wide,
"is one this size to lure myself a really willing bride!"

And so he set out searching, and although it seemed too heavy,
he found himself an iron bigger than the biggest Chevy,
He chipped away beneath it to make room for a fuel sledge,
and as that giant weight began to teeter on the edge,

his patience finally ended and he gave a little shove,
and down it came and buried John 'neath Heaven from above.

And the moral of the story for you, listener, so patient,
is to recognize the value of these rocks that are so ancient.
For many of the smallest are among the most profound,
and it's better to collect those than be crushed into the ground.

Ralph Harvey,
Antarctica

Bushfire Simulation, Adelaide Hills

*Reimagining the work of Dr Mika Peace, Australian Fire
Research Meteorologist*

Monday sees the mathematician
seeding her model with soft mouse clicks, sowing
artificial scarps with drought-affected fuel:

long-leaf box, grey ribbon gum, silky guinea flower greening
below the overstorey. Nine black cockatoos
glide south, automata burning out in a blank blue screen.

Tuesday sets westerlies amongst the numbers.
The mathematician takes note as the heads of twos, threes and sevens
snap back, whipsawed. She bends to her display

and begins the run. All that Wednesday, the black box shuttles
flames about, hand over fist, scattering
stand-ins like silverfish in the light

before Thursday's smoke plume, at first lavish and white
then bruising and dense as a summer crush
curdles and sets, its gargantuan

base spinning counter to the crown, the base and the crown
both now overwriting
near-surface winds and the sun, a dreadful shade

purging paddocks of shadows and smothering
the urge to run. Until, on Friday,
spotting sets off

inside a small gridded cube—firebrands as bits as pixels
announcing the front in ropy, self-iterating
strands—an ember storm lofting long ribbon-bark fuels venting,

still burning away from turbulent knots
and into errant gully winds,
to where they lodge at last in our roof cavities like clouds

of homing bees. *I have come a long way,*
she thinks in the reddening light of the last time-step,
to sift mimicries of ash and fumes.

To cast, with soft mouse clicks
and with some newfangled capnomancy,
runnels of molten car parts

into cool key findings. Such a long way, she thinks,
to write down these smooth and edifying texts—lessons
for a calculable world.

EJ Baird,
Tasmania, Australia

Círculo polar

Alto y ventoso círculo polar antártico
glaciares que sobrevuelan los cormoranes
en impoluto hielo y su manto de albura.
La ballena azul y el legendario kráken
navegan sin pausa el solsticio de verano.

Témpanos que me llevan a Patagonia
Finis Terrae, azul pacífico salpicado
australidad de embarcaciones y naufragios
ignoto laberinto de mares, islas y fiordos.

Tierra del Fuego al sur del mundo
tribus perdidas de yaganes y selk´nam
                    ¡extintos…!
sus fantasmas de humo y niebla
caminan hoy sobre lagos de hielo.

Bajo la bóveda de astros sigo la senda
historia épica narrada en petroglifos,
viento que me deja palpar sus presencias
pasos, rostros y voces que me rodean.

Enciendo el fulgor de la antorcha
el mural documenta su genealogía,
pongo mis manos sobre las suyas
pintadas en las cuevas que habitaron.

Aquí, donde rugen los volcanes
iluminando laderas de araucarias
con su rojo flujo de lava candente
otorgando nuevas formas al paisaje.

Emerge tectónica la cordillera andina
portentosa columna vertebral de América.

Theodoro Elssaca,
Santiago de Chile

Our World

I hear century after century
what cannot be imagined
cannot be. The wind, ice and fire
its constant companions, ever
wanting to make a language
full of light, full of dark.
They are are a pure act of nature,
the deep down mother of us all.
She is ever desiring words to tell
us how it is we are so mysterious
to ourselves and to the world.
Our world is what it is. The World
itself is a Word. Hope is a thing
that perches in the Soul.

Michael Harlow,
New Zealand

Links for further engagement with the poets in this anthology:

The Polaris Trilogy 1

Rock

Margaret Brand
https://en-gb.facebook.com/mbrandart

Norbert Góra
 https://www.facebook.com/norbert.gora.94

Maid Čorbić
 https://www.facebook.com/xcelendge

Helen Cova
https://www.helencova.com/

Emilie Bilman
https://emiliebilman.wixsite.com/emily-bilman

Xe M. Sánchez
 https://wildcourt.co.uk/?s=xe+m.+sanchez

Water

Steven OBrien
https://thelondonmagazine.org/staff/steven-obrien/

Gabriele Glang
http://gabrieleglang.de

Londeka Mdluli
https://www.researchgate.net/profile/Londeka-Mdluli

Widaad Pangarker
https://www.instagram.com/widwords/

Suzanne van Leendert
suzanne@uandeyemedia.nl

Ndaba Sibanda
https://m.youtube.com/watch?v=Hn_JxOh25eU

Catherine Aubelle
https://www.aubelle-cath.com/about-me/

Daniel Moreschi
https://www.instagram.com/daniel.moreschi/

Nadia Ibrashi
https://www.narrativemagazine.com/authors/nadia-ibrashi

Ian Aitken
https://www.ianaitken.com/bio

Alshaad Kara
https://thesuburbanreview.com/2022/04/29/qa-alshaad-kara/

Yogesh Patel
https://writersmosaic.org.uk/wp-content/uploads/2021/05/Yogesh-Patel-The-torn-worlds-basted-through-my-poems.pdf

Air

Jane Dougherty
https://janedougherty.wordpress.com/

Trish Bennett
http://trishbennettwriter.com/

Lily Prigioniero
https://www.pw.org/directory/writers/lily_prigioniero

Christian Ward
https://www.facebook.com/fightingcancerwithpoetry/

David Dephy
https://internetpoem.com/david-dephy/

María Ángeles Pérez López
https://www.youtube.com/watch?v=glbQevdOKYs

Svenja Grabner
https://www.svenjagrabner.at/

Patricia Devlin-Hill
 https://tinyurl.com/282xmese

Gaetano Longo
http://1.svp.org.mk/poets/gaetano-longo/?lang=en

Spinning Together

Manja Maksimovič
https://manjameximexcessive6.wordpress.com/category/napowrimo-2022/

Ingrid Wilson
https://experimentsinfiction.com/

M Ait Ali
 https://www.goodreads.com/author/show/18447060.M_Ait_Ali

Daisy Blacklock
https://twitter.com/daisy_blacklock

Byron Beynon
 https://sway.office.com/7FbywUGdP4eLTivy?ref=Link

Helmuth Haberkamm
http://www.helmuthaberkamm.de/

Norbert Krapf
http://www.krapfpoetry.net/

Amalou Ouassou
https://afanine.net/00003/

The Polaris Trilogy2

Stars

Kerfe Roig
https://kblog.blog/

Elise Paschen
https://www.poetryfoundation.org/poets/elise-paschen

Kathryn Sadakierski
https://www.pw.org/directory/writers/kathryn_sadakierski

Hunter Liguore
http:/www.hungerliguore.org

Neethu Krishnan
https://www.instagram.com/neethu.krishnan_/

Daniela Gioseffi
https://poets.org/poet/daniela-gioseffi

Fernando Cabrera
https://www.facebook.com/Fernando.CabreraReynoso

Max Henderson
https://www.linkedin.com/mwlite/in/max-henderson-5196a543

Lali Tsipi Michaeli
https://en.wikipedia.org/wiki/Lali_Tsipi_Michaeli

Shonda Buchanan
http://www.shondabuchanan.com/

Oceana Rain Stuart
https://www.oceanarainstuart.com/about-the-artist

Rolando Kattan
 https://twitter.com/RolandoKattan

Ted Kooser
 https://www.tedkooser.net/

Sun

Carl Boon
https://www.thenasiona.com/2020/09/04/episode-32-imaginative-biography-places-names/

Stephanie Harper
http://slharperpoetry.com/

Sally Ashton
https://sallyashton.com/

Sara Cahill Marron
https://www.saracahillmarron.com/

Moon

Daisy Bassen
 https://daisybassen.com/

Jenny Kalahar
 https://twitter.com/jennybookseller

Linda Neal Reising
https://open.spotify.com/episode/0UZy3VXaF6FH1uAnzw1V3w

Humberto Quintanar
https://eln0voescritoralqu1m157a.blogspot.com/
Joann Balingit
http://joannbalingit.org/

Lucy Park
http://www.sijo.org/

Charlotte Yeung
https://cmyeung.wixsite.com/website/about

Marjorie Maddox Hafer
http://marjoriemaddox.com/

Elizabeth Jorgensen
https://lizjorgensen.weebly.com/sijo.html

Rei Berroa
https://mcl.gmu.edu/people/rberroa

Marianne Boruch
https://www.poetryfoundation.org/poets/marianne-boruch

Dana Gelinas
https://conexos.org/2013/02/10/interstate-35-highway-y-otros-poemas/

Héctor Carreto
https://www.darklight.nyc/hctor-carreto

Walter Bargen
https://www.poetryfoundation.org/poets/walter-bargen

Akshaya Pawaskar
https://www.instagram.com/akshaya_pawaskar/

Angela Acosta

https://www.pw.org/directory/writers/angela_acosta

Mary Sexson
http://masexson.wordpress.com/
Nancy Jorgensen
https://nancyjorgensen.weebly.com/

Megha Sood
https://meghasworldsite.wordpress.com/about/

José Luis Vega
https://en.wikipedia.org/wiki/Jose_Luis_Vega

Robert Okaji
https://robertokaji.com/

Michelle Beauchamp
https://mishunderstood.wordpress.com/

Diane DeCillis
http://dianedecillis.com/

Kelly Kaur
http://kellykaur.com/

Cynthia Gallaher
https://linktr.ee/cynthiagallaher

Mike Nierste
https://issuu.com/mikenierste

Together In The Sky

Jennifer Barricklow
https://dailycompost.wordpress.com/

Flor Aguilera
https://es.wikipedia.org/wiki/Flor_Aguilera

Felicia Sanzari Chernesky
https://www.facebook.com/feliciasanzarichernesky

Diane Raptosh
http://dianeraptoshcom

Carolyn Kreiter-Foronda
http://carolynforonda.com/

Jessica Thompson
https://www.pw.org/directory/writers/jessica_d_thompson

D.C. Houston
https://www.instagram.com/d.c.houston

R. Bremner
https://www.youtube.com/watch?v=EGbY4ec8Ius&t=1190s

Lynne Burnett
http://lynneburnett.ca/

Tom Chandler
http://tomchandlerpoet.com/

Denise Lajimodiere
https://www.deniselajimodiere.com/

Carl Scharwath
https://m.facebook.com/100000485098479/

Changming Yuan
https://poetryinvoice.ca/read/poets/changming-yuan

Anita Nahal
http://anitanahal.com/

Indran Amirthanaya
https:// youtube.com/indranam

Louise Dupré
https://en.wikipedia.org/wiki/Louise_Dupre

Smeetha Bhoumik
https://yugenquestreview.in/craft-unravelling-the-sestina-as-a-magic-bridge-by-smeetha-bhoumik/

Patricia F. Clark
https://patriciafclark.com/

Ninot Aziz
https://twitter.com/ninotaziz

Ruthelen Burns
https://www.loc.gov/item/2021688038/

Rob Omura
http://poemsniederngasse.com/Poetry/084_omura.html

Matthew Graham
https://www.in.gov/arts/programs-and-services/partners/indiana-poet-laureate/

Fernando Operé
https://www.operesantillana.com/

Sandra Alcosser
https://mfa.sdsu.edu/faculty/alcosser

Eugenia Nájera Verástegui
https://especulativas.com/2022/02/28/eugenia-najera-verastegui-almas/

David Evans
 https://ericedits.wordpress.com/2007/10/19/interview-with-a-poet-sd-poet-laureate-david-evans/

Rhina P. Espaillat
https://www.poetryfoundation.org/poets/rhina-p-espaillat

Larry Wiowode
https://www.americamagazine.org/arts-culture/2022/05/24/cbc-column

The Polaris Trilogy 3

Ice

Luis Cruz
https://fb.watch/hDsoAB2B9G/

Alan Lake
https://www.facebook.com/allan.lake

Catherine Corrigan
https://usasciencefestival.org/people/dr-catherine-corrigan/

Wind

Anne Casey
http://www.anne-casey.com/

Doug Jacquier
https://sixcrookedhighwaysblog.wordpress.com/about/

Judith Crispin
https://judithcrispin.com/

Fire

María Alejandra Fumaroni

https://iccglobal.org/2021/04/01/icc-food-memories-empanadas-and-falafel/

John Kennedy
https://m.facebook.com/story.php?story_fbid=pfbid02VcxbuhurdVcPiymK4zUobwxfuYm7sh2x7v7HzwqMfVdCU42QfM7ta96xcTS6oVVvl&id=731005806&mibextid=Nif5oz

Jorge William Tigrero Vaca
https://instagram.com/jtigrerov

Gabriel Chávez Casazola
 https://circulodepoesia.com/2017/10/poemas-de-gabriel-chavez-casazola/

Together On Earth

Mariana Orrego Serna
https://www.instagram.com/marsol.omgaia

Claire Bridge
https://www.clairebridgeartist.com/

Alex Bassett
https://twitter.com/alexkbassett

EJ Baird
https://ejbaird.com/

Theodoro Elssaca
https://elssaca.cl/conversacion-con-theodoro-elssaca/

Michael Harlow
https://acortar.link/KrbIBy

Made in the USA
Monee, IL
29 January 2023

26676050R00125